Wind, Waves, and a Suicidal Boat

≈

Personal stories from the most dangerous job in the world

By

Chris White

WIND, WAVES, AND A SUICIDAL BOAT

Library of Congress Catalog Control Number: 2001119501

ISBN: 0-7596-8820-6

This book is printed with soy ink on acid free paper.

Published by:
Black Spruce Press
1466 Janish Dr.
Sandpoint, ID 83864
***

TO SHARA WHITE:
SOUL FRIEND, PARTNER IN ADVENTURE, FORGIVING, AND NEVER WHINES

ALASKA

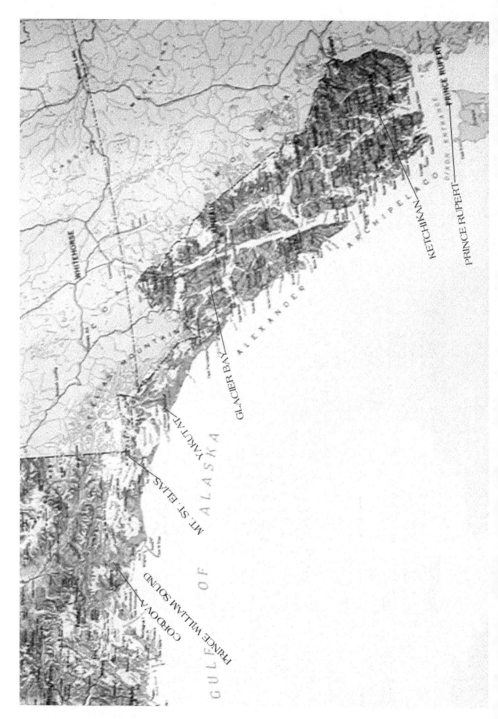

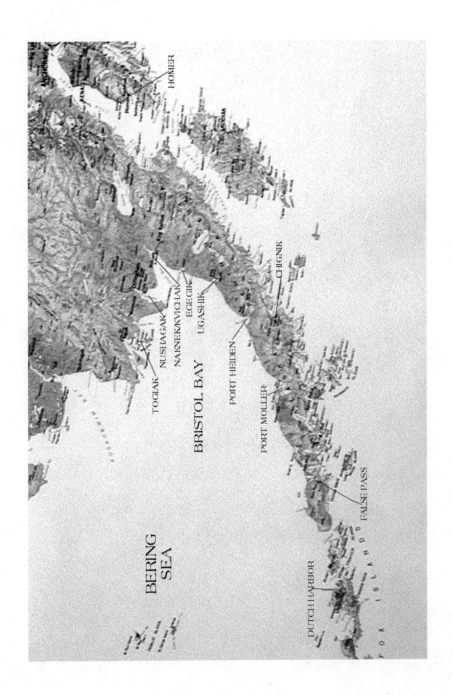

BERING
SEA

BRISTOL BAY

HOMER

CHIGNIK

UGASHIK

EGEGIK

NAKNEK/KVICHAK

NUSHAGAK

TOGIAK

PORT HEIDEN

PORT MOLLER

FALSE PASS

DUTCH HARBOR

CONTENTS

PHOTOS

Unless otherwise noted, all photos by Chris White.

Cover photo by Mike Reitz: Bay Rose taking a pounding in the Nushagak river.

APPRECIATION

I would like to thank a number of people from my heart for the energy they have spent in helping to bring this book to life.

It is a writers' bane to be so involved in a story that it becomes extremely difficult to see the problems and mistakes that are inevitably there. An honest critic is invaluable.

Special thanks to Whit Deschner, Joe Upton, Robert Perkins, and Shara White, and Rita Hutchens, for their extra effort and invaluable contributions.

For their time and constructive observations, thank you Joe Harris, Frederic Wiedemann, David Sawyer, Trip Quillman, Eileen Doyle, Tina Friedman, Larry White, Janie White, and Barbara Tilley.

Thank you John van Amerongen for publishing pieces of my work.

Thanks Mike Reitz for the cover photo and years of fishing together. Also Bob Haynes, I was lucky he was my first skipper.

And thanks to people like Tom Hutton who said, "Hey, write that stuff down."

The teachers in my life have been numerous. Many have no idea of the role they played in offering me valuable lessons; I honor each one of them.

In particular, I want to apologize to the fellow with the premature mustache in seventh grade that I punched in the nose for no good reason. Also, the two women at Outward Bound whose certificates I withheld because they didn't meet my expectations. I was wrong in all cases. I am grateful for them helping me learn about compassion.

DISCLAIMER

On surface these stories are meant to entertain, and hopefully amuse. Most of them involve risk. I admit it is another intention of mine to urge the reader to TRY THIS AT HOME. Why? Because each of us has his/her own path, and they all involve risk—that is how we grow in the adventure that is life, and I don't believe anyone's journey really ends until we ALL arrive.

The risk possibilities are endless. For some it might be a simple kind word to a stranger; for others discovering the cause and then letting go of long held, but cancerous, anger; still, for others it might be facing a raging river. For mankind, it might be risking peace instead of war.

When risk-taking involves physical danger, there are reasonable and unreasonable risks...I am guilty of both. It _may_ be that your grand adventure is to live life paralyzed in a wheelchair from a risk that went wrong, but please remember that you always have a CHOICE, and that is your responsibility alone.

**WE HAVE THE ADVENTURE FOR WHICH
WE ARE READY**

—Joseph Campbell

PROLOGUE

RISKING FOR YOUR LIFE

≈

If you want to be brave and reach for the top of the sky, and the farthest point on the horizon, and you know who you'll meet there: Great soldiers and seafarers, artists and dreamers who need to be close to the light. They need to be in danger of burning by fire—and I want to get there.

—Carly Simon, *Touched by the Sun*

•

Late one winter, in my twenties, I landed back in Fairbanks after a thirty-day solo adventure in northern Alaska's Brooks Range. I was different after my vision quest: more confident, more appreciative of our planet's fragile beauty and, to the point here, determined not to linger on the safe side of life.

One of the issues I had grappled was the question of freedom versus security. For me, this was one of the most frightening contemplations because the path of freedom, which I partially define as the authentic road of one's highest purpose, frequently requires a step into the unknown, a leap of faith. I had come to realize that I was not really free. I was, in fact, imprisoned by my assorted fears and the illusion of who I thought I was. I hated this. I sensed that real freedom lay stalking straight down the throat of these fears. For me, facing this darkness skulking in the backstage of my daily life would become a prime focus that remains even today in its ever evolving form.

In activating my quest, I committed myself to discovering what was over the edge of the horizons I had so longingly gazed at while standing by the oceans of my youth. More than a quest for the adrenaline rush inherent in risk-taking, I was eager to taste the marrow of life's mystery, find my physical limitations, and the real measure of my mental and emotional fiber. Unclear to me, my journey ahead, while outward in appearance, was really about an inner journey. It slowly revealed itself as an adventure of the soul, whose vast dimensions and wonders I could not imagine at the time. My particular classrooms were the oceans, mountains and rivers, but the greatest teacher was risk itself. The true stories told here, intertwined with my work as a commercial fisherman, are parts of that journey.

•

My particular affliction was an addiction to the lure and challenge of the overgrown, dark trail—not always the smartest, and rarely the safest. Thus, you, dear reader, might determine that some of the life-threatening experiences described in this book were foolishly sought, perhaps unnecessary acts of lunacy easily avoided—and you could be right! But there are good reasons behind the madness of risk-takers—whether challenging the Everests of nature, a new job, or the myriad passageways of committing (or un-committing) to a relationship. For some, it is challenge enough getting out of bed each morning. At root for everyone who accepts risk is the belief that exploring the infinite wonders life has to offer is greater than the fear of failure.

Each person's path of letting go and leaving the known is highly individualized. Risk, in whatever form, is merely the vehicle. Still, each is answering an ancient evolutionary call programmed into our DNA to help us answer the critical questions in life—a summons to find meaning, the value of Self and our place and purpose in the Great Mystery.

As a society, we spend huge amounts of time and energy shielding ourselves from failure, pain and death. We heavily invest in fear, at the expense of our freedom. Compare this to the epitome of pure risk taking: a child striving to take its first step. We see fearless courage in the face of unstoppable curiosity. Here is pure desire to explore and know more.

Unlike the child, in addition to our societal agreement on death, we carry personal learned fears scattered before us. They obscure the trail like downed limbs after a storm. The fear is frequently born trying to measure-up to the demanding expectations of others—and ourselves. We fear failure; we fear all loss; we fear all pain; we fear humiliation; we fear judgment. But even in the face of these formidable forces, how can we deny our life force and squander the incredible opportunities life offers to feel alive? Without taking risks, how else can we plumb the depths, leave the safe and secure, shatter the illusions of who we think we are, and discover our authentic selves? How can we not want to look over the edge? How tragic to arrive at the conclusion of this life burdened with regrets for not having tried. Overcoming the prison of fears that stifle our evolution and keep us from our highest purpose is not for the faint-hearted, but it *is* the Real game. The sweet reward on the other side of fear is the love and joy we crave.

•

> To put meaning in one's life may end in madness. But life without meaning is the torture of restlessness and vague desire. It is a boat longing for the sea and yet afraid.
> —Edgar Lee Masters

Risk-taking at a young age is like working-out and gradually building muscles—baby steps that start on the surface and move deeper over time into wisdom. Unfortunately, our over-protective culture has effectively robbed our youth. Young men particularly lack the opportunities to discover the unique strengths and weaknesses of their mental fortitude, emotional maturity, and moral integrity. The initiations of manhood carried on by more 'primitive' societies—the rites, walkabouts and vision quests—that help determine and build a young man's character, are largely missing in our 'civilized' world. War, in its 'righteousness', was once considered an acceptable proving ground. Today its technological remoteness, blurry reasoning (except in extreme cases), and accountable suffering viewed from an evolving higher consciousness, have rightly proven it a wholly unsatisfactory means of achieving manhood.

•

The Dalai Lama said, "Great love and achievements take great risk." In my career as an Outward Bound instructor, part of my greatest satisfaction was observing the faces of students who persevered over difficulties. Having gained the top of a difficult rock climb, or crossed a frightening ropes-course obstacle, they beamed with newfound determination and an awareness of their untapped potential. There was a palpable, powerful energy emanating from having overcome their fear. The success boosted confidence that flowed into all areas of their lives.

So, what of the inevitable failures? One of the many I have had to face was when I was attempting to save my father's sailboat in "A Mariner's Nightmare". I was so stricken with the terrifying burden of the potential loss of his boat (*strangely, not our lives*), my mind narrowed to encompass only the immediate things that could be done to survive. Yet, in the stress of those moments I could not remember where the lifejackets were, despite the fact I had previously stowed them in easy reach under a cockpit hatch.

The irony is that breakdowns do lead to breakthroughs. Protective shields shatter when we already have a bloody nose. We are plagued by copious amounts of delusion as it is. These false gods wrongly anchor us in the natural current of our true purpose. Knowing our weaknesses through failure helps us pull that anchor and move on with the current toward our purpose.

The gains acquired as a result of risk-taking soften the pain of failure or mistakes. The whole journey is more important then the parts. Further, in failure is born humility, which teaches us critical lessons in understanding and compassion for the shortfalls we all suffer.

•

The metaphysical mysteries unfolding in the wake of my own risk-taking amazed me. I do not give much credence to religions. They tend to separate us with dogma and decree that fosters an unconscious we-vs-them mentality. True healthy spirituality recognizes our essential oneness with each other and non-judgmentally embraces our differences. My cathedral is outside, and I do not need an interpreter for communication with Spirit.

When I pushed hard for answers (like a child tearing apart a toy to see how it works), demanding understanding and vision, I sometimes received very clear responses. Paragliding off a mountaintop, I once completely collapsed (stalled) my wing and plummeted from treetop level 50-feet straight down to the hard-packed snow. I should have been seriously injured; instead, my body was badly shocked, but I walked away! A clear voice in my head said, *your continued stubbornness taxes and amuses us, but if it is proof of our love and protection you seek, then that is what you will get.* I eventually 'got' the message and was able to release much of the gripping fear of failure and death. I understood each not as an end, but a rebirth. To my surprise, gaining strength and confidence allowed me to ease the control I had been holding onto so tenaciously. The faith and trust that took its place brought the seeming miracles, the unexpected support, and the unexplained survival.

•

Risking revealed a sweet consciousness of the unity we all share on the planet, and the cosmos beyond. I saw this in the eyes of my students after their three-day solo—time totally alone in the wilderness with minimum comforts and devoid of man-made distractions. Finding empowerment from surviving their demons, their eyes invariably reflected a visible clarity. The experience revealed new inner strength that tapped into a unifying thread connecting us all with support, love and compassion. They discovered that humans are at their best when cooperating and working together for the whole. That is the souls journey; excessive self-serving individualism is misguided ego. The theme of their common epiphany was: *while being so alone, being _truly_ alone was an illusion.*

I imagine all of us on the outside of a great circle, each in a slightly different spot, trying to get to the center. In the center are the states of consciousness mirroring 'enlightenment', 'self-realization' or 'love' in some form or another. Risk moves us towards the center, and the closer we get, the more unified we become.

•

Once we take a risk and leave the safety of our controlled environment, we can never be the same again. For me, searching for undiscovered places led me back Home again. I am left with a deeply grateful appreciation for each wondrous moment. It has become clear that the thousands of outward miles traveled on the quest have been about gaining the strength and wisdom to travel the inner twenty-inches from my head to my heart.

CHAPTER 1

WIND, WAVES, AND A SUICIDAL BOAT

≈

The person who has made one hundred mistakes knows far more than the person who has made none.

—Some wise person

•

Incredibly, Shar was still clinging to the bow of the heaving boat, sprawled out like a cat on a steep, steel roof. Disappearing underwater for the third time, my wife emerged with the green wave cascading off her body, her death-grip on the anchor line intact, yelling something I couldn't quite hear. Her words flew by, mixed in the cacophony of breaking waves and the howling wind. Sputtering, she yelled again, "SLACK, I NEED MORE SLACK ON THE ANCHOR!"

This time I heard most of it. I gave *Rebel*, our leased fishing boat, full power and prayed this wouldn't be the moment the vessel succeeded in its single-minded suicidal efforts. The boat's methods were many. As the water dumped over us, thrashing us like a chip of wood in a washing machine, it was obvious *Rebel's* intention this time was to drown herself. The obituary would read: *strangled at the end of a taut anchor line*— a savage termination of the troublesome albatross the boat had become to us.

•

1

We were literally immersed in another hard lesson handed to us during the 1977 Bristol Bay commercial salmon season in Alaska. The Bay, tucked into the southeast corner of the Bering Sea, is home to all five species of pacific salmon, and the world's greatest sockeye salmon run. We had entered the fishery with just enough fishing experience to know what to do but, evidently, not enough to stay out of trouble. Proof of this was pummeling us now. In the deceptive calm of low tide, I had anchored in the middle of Egegik's notorious Coffee Point tide-rip. When the 26-foot tide flooded in with the force of a raging river, and the wind resumed its gale force, I cursed myself for putting us in this position, especially aboard a totally unreliable vessel that carried a death-wish like a banner of honor.

Originally I was looking for independence, adventure and the romance of the seas. Yes, there was adventure everywhere, but I hadn't expected to find it so fraught with potential harm (made all the more so by *Rebel's* intent.)

Peering through the stinging deluge, I glimpsed Shar again struggle to her knees for better leverage. The furious assault of the wind ripped at her rain gear and threatened to send her soaring naked with the seagulls. The romance I sought was far from this reality. Instead, I thought, *what a damn good sport she is to be up there!*

•

Our search for our own commercial fishing operation led us to stake our claim in Bristol Bay, a carefully managed, 'clean' fishery. Clean meant we would not be catching species other than targeted salmon. *Wild*, organic salmon, not drugged and dyed weaklings from caged fish farms. God made the place for salmon, the indigenous people, and fewer numbered white folks who like the unharnessed, stark beauty of life in the tundra. The first requirement is to be hardy enough to endure the cold, dark winters.

Each year an average of 164 million salmon return to the clear, cold waters of Alaska, completing a boggling navigational feat that exceeds 2000 miles round-trip. The swimming hordes celebrate the end of their cycle in one of the most extraordinary spawning orgies on the planet. The price for their once-in-a-lifetime sexcapade is steep: death for all participants after the last orgasmic shudder has subsided and the eggs of future generations are safely buried in the stream bottoms.

•

Over the winter we had scraped together all the money we had to buy the necessary limited-entry permit. Left with empty pockets and anxious optimism, nothing remained for the all-important boat from which to launch our new business. At the time, paying 25% of our catch to lease a vessel for the year seemed a reasonable alternative.

In early June we arrived on the windswept Egegik beach to look at the fishing vessel *Rebel* for the first time. If the fish arrived on time, and they rarely missed the fourth-of-July peak by more then two days, we hopefully had plenty of time to get things shipshape. We stood funeral-like before the boat, bowed and silent with hands clasped, our somber posture reflecting the grim scene before us. I observed what looked like a very large coffin sunk deeply into the sand. It was currently serving as a dumpster. Here and there was visible evidence that, yes, a wooden boat existed under the garbage. With its propeller buried, it projected an attitude of a stubborn dog hunkered down in the sand, serenely content, and unwilling to move. Its age was undeterminable beyond the fact that plywood had probably not been around long when it was built. I could almost hear *Rebel* announce, *I'm done with my life on the sea. Don't even THINK of trying to end my retirement.*

I inched forward, half expecting some living thing to leap out, and peeked over the splintered gunwale to confirm the claim it was equipped with a gas engine. I could only assume the rusted hunk of metal hidden in the shadows of the strewn flotsam was it. There was a small cuddy cabin forward that sported its own moss garden, and obviously received enough water through the deck above to keep it healthy. (Unbeknown to us, the boat had sunk the year before and been left to rot in the corrosive salt that had coated everything.) Looking at the swamp-like dampness on the bunks, it was clear we would sleep in a shack on the bluff above the beach during closures.

3

Wind, Waves, and a Suicidal Boat

Backing slowly away from the foreboding scene, I was thinking that the task before us appeared to be approaching the impossible realms. Shar, mirroring my thoughts, said, "It will be a miracle if we can get it fishing."

Miracle indeed! At this point in life my mechanical skills sputtered out right after oil changes. As grim as the situation looked, we had no other options at hand.

•

De-rusting spray was the scent of the day. By the end of the week, with both of us working 18-20 hour days, my mechanical abilities had broadened exponentially. Shar had the deck sealed, the boat painted, and our three shackles of two by fifty fathom (12 by 300 feet) gillnets hung.

The glittering star sustaining my bright outlook was a wooden crate sitting next to the boat. It contained a brand new transmission. The gear's fresh factory paint stood in stark contrast to the mass of rusted machinery that adorned the *Rebel*. Each day the crate took on a more magical proportion until I was sure it would answer all our problems and become a major factor in our success, somehow gluing the whole ugly package together. I held fast to the owner's encouraging words how, when I installed the gear, "She ought to go real good." Digging the sand away from the propeller, I peered under at what looked suspiciously like the fan blade from a car radiator, only smaller. I reflected on the small and extremely fast turning props driving high-speed hydroplanes. With the new gear ratio on the transmission, plus *Rebel's* flat bottom, I heartily agreed that, "She ought to go real good." In my deepest delusions I imagined this baby might even scream!

And scream she did! Actually, it was more like the agonizing roar of an awakened angry animal when the engine miraculously started. The motor had no muffler and easily drowned out our joyous exclamations.

"We'll have to scrounge a muffler somewhere," I yelled in Shar's face to penetrate the fingers stuffed into her ears.

"I think, Dr. Frankenstein," she yelled back, "silencing this monster you've brought to life may be the least of our worries."

4

Three days later, and only with heroic effort—a pickup truck intermittently towing and pushing *Rebel's* twenty-six feet over rolling logs—were we able to launch the reluctant boat into the surf. I could not shake the stubborn dog image and imagined us forcing it, snarling and snapping, into a bath it loathed.

As usual, it was blowing onshore from the South, producing pounding surf that made boarding the boat a frantic exercise. "Go for it." I urged, boosting Shar over the rail and throwing myself in after her. I landed on top, both of us soaked, our hip boots full of water and useless. Pouring out her boots, Shar declared, "This is going to get old very fast if we have to do *this* everyday."

When *Rebel* hit the water, I felt the strong pull from the huge tidal respirations of the Bering Sea (frequently over 23 feet of tide change), but at this moment I was focused on seeing how fast the boat would go. We poured a quick ceremonial shot of rum into the sea and, after Shar intoned an appropriate incantation, I fired up the engine.

In case there arose a need to drift back, I prudently decided to run against the current. I scoffed at the five-knot tide we would buck. Surely, when we broke the surface tension and started high-speed planing, the rushing tide would disappear in a plume of spray, the wind in our hair would blow away the last lingering doubts. Wild-eyed with anticipation, I turned to Shar and issued my first command: "Hold on matey, brace for the thrust!"

I engaged the new gear and inched the throttle forward to its estimated three-quarter's position. The responding roar of the engine was spine-tingling thrilling, however, I was not feeling the corresponding forward leap of the boat. I glanced at the shore and noted we were still going backwards with the tide! In answer to Shar's sarcastic comments about the severe G-forces she was experiencing, I jammed the throttle wide open. The noise rivaled the space shuttle takeoff; our seven-knot top speed barely beat the tide—but not by much. We discovered that, with any breeze blowing on the side, the boat did not have the power, or rudder, to turn us through the wind when going left. Hence, if we wanted to change course 100-degrees to port (left), we were frequently required to circle 260-degrees in the opposite direction to gain the desired heading.

In response to a sloshing noise, I looked down to see the floorboards under our feet starting to float. I suddenly felt vulnerable and wished our equipment was more sophisticated than a hand-held compass, a portable CB radio, and the sailboat oar that acted as our depth finder.

Rebel was starting her tricks and had disabled the bilge pump needed to stem the water coming through the seams. The hull leaked freely and, though the leaks in time would diminish with swelling, the engine's salt water cooling-pump had become a berserk fountain and was blasting water everywhere. We bailed feverishly while I reflected on the true nature of the dysfunctional relationship we would have with this seemingly black-hearted beast.

By evening we had everything repaired. We tied the boat to the continuous running-line—resembling a clothesline looped between the shore and an outer mooring. Standing on the beach we hauled the boat out to the safety of deep water—and our exhausted selves up the bluff to bed.

After our wild boarding drill in the surf the next morning, we set off to explore the boundaries of the Egegik district we were committed to fish. (One can change districts after registering and not fishing for 48 hours). Of the five districts available to fish, this was the most manageable one—not that I would have dared venture much past yelling distance from shore with *Rebel.*

Sniffing out the corners of Egegik would have been easier had we a chart to follow, so much of our exploration was in braille. Eventually we formed an idea of the shape of things, deciding to stay within radio range and concentrate on a five-mile drift along the north beach. Eager and ready for our first set, a small hydraulic pump spun the stern roller that fed our three shackles over the stern, and away we drifted with the out-going tide. We drifted back in the evening with two fish.

We only caught seven the next day, thanks to *Rebel.* The engine died after the first set from a sludge plugged fuel line.

I called into the radio, "*Lulu, Lulu,* do you pick me up on this channel, Tommy?"

"Yo, I'm here," his reassuring voice came back.

"*Rebel's* choked herself comatose. Can you tow us in?"

"Sure," he said and added, "You'll need to watch that boat carefully. There is a confirmed history of psychotic behavior."

"Roger on that, thanks for the warning.", I didn't dare ask about the psychotic condition of past captains.

We grounded *Rebel* on the beach during the falling night tide. It was early morning by the time I had removed the fuel tank and cleaned-out the water and gunk. Shar had been equally busy repairing the ugly, whale-size hole I had torn in the net when I cleverly caught an anchored boat on the drift out. We re-launched with the aid of many kind people helping to push the boat out into the wind and waves. We drifted back again in an embarrassingly short time...I had forgotten to re-open the fuel valve.

•

The fishing picked-up late in June for most of the fleet. The Department of Fish and Game was granting 12 hours of fishing a day to allow enough salmon to move upstream and spawn. We, too, were swept up in the increasing pulse of activity and anticipated an exciting fish-filled week. On Monday, as the skirts of dawn lifted signaling the end of the four-hour northern night, I looked out the window to find *Rebel* gone! Gnawing through the running line, she had bolted on a rising tide— successful in her first escape. Three hours later we found her hugging the pilings, high on the rocks under one of the upriver canneries. She looked disappointed at her discovery. Luckily, I smelled the additional booby trap she'd set: 15 gallons of gas snuck into the bilge, hoping to blow us all to flaming bits when I sparked the starter.

My attitude toward the *Rebel* was growing more callous by the day. The boat clearly had a serious death wish and was going about her penchant for killing herself in a baffling multitude of ways. I, on the other hand, desired that the vessel do its job and carry us through the fishing season alive—though I had let go of any hope of doing so in style. There seemed to be very little the boat and I could agree on in this area.

•

There was other drama happening. I had arrived at my first commercial sea command posturing as if I had graduated from the Captain Bligh School-of-Captaining. The school's creed declared: *the more unsure and anxious you are in a situation, the louder you should yell*. This was <u>not</u> the school from which Shar graduated. The problem was compounded when I took things close to the edge, like drifting down on a shore setnet (a shorter net anchored at both ends and tended from shore), while ignoring her warnings of the ensuing catastrophe. Hoping that I could pull out a miraculous recovery in the end and regain her confidence, I ignored her. Later, I had to endure her disgusted looks during the two-hour ordeal required to disentangle us from the setnet. I soon decided it best to change my attitude, burn my diploma, and most of all, avoid an embarrassing mutiny.

•

Three days after the escape, the engine over-heated and quit as we tried to power ourselves off one of the many sand flats. *Rebel* had successfully sucked enough muck into the cooling system to gag herself into unconsciousness. When the tide receded, we were beached high on the bar with 300 salmon caught in the net stretched out in the sand behind us.

"The fishing period ends in two hours." Shar observed. "Wonder if the fish cops will show any mercy toward two rookies with a handicapped boat and the net still out after the closure?"

Before I could reply how any judge would be reduced to tears after our tale about the boat, she was over the side and trudging across the sand to inquire at another boat stuck on the same bar a half-mile away. The information she received was not encouraging. Choosing to avoid the stiff fine, and an early reputation of lawlessness, we picked the fish and slogged them back to the boat. Then, with sweat-drenching exertion, we dragged the net's 600 pounds of dead weight across the sand and over the stern. *Rebel* sat quiet and placidly smug, hydraulics useless, as we suffered in our manual labor. Purging the sand out of the system took more time then we had. With the tide rushing in we called for another tow from our patient fishing partners.

A day later I thought *Rebel* had escaped again but, upon closer inspection, realized she'd jerked the mooring anchor out and now lay high above the tide-line directly below us. She had managed to impale herself on a rock and bend her rudder in the process. We missed another period of fishing making repairs. To cap the day, we holed her again with the truck trying to push her back into the water.

I slumped on the sand, nearing the end of my rope. "I hope we make enough this season for the hefty dose of repair I'll need after all this. I'm spinning into a spiritual void."

"<u>This</u> from Mister *'that which does not kill me, strengthens me'*?" Shar observed while stroking my head. "Why, if Nietzsche is right, you'll be Superman when this is over."

•

The following weeks consisted of sporadic fishing between boat resuscitation drills, and our fifth tow. Mechanically, the cooling pump choked to death, the inner guts of the steering system disintegrated, and the first starter finally burned up. Structurally, another boat put a large hole in our bow. Circumstantially, *Rebel* broke the mooring block twice during attempted escapes, and I wrapped the net around an anchored boat and still *another* setnet site. The leaks grew worse. We made repairs as best we could. Mentally—we staggered on.

•

9

Rebel, discovered by the author impaled on a rock after another escape.

(photo by Shar White)

Shar, doing what she loves.

Early one morning in July, we finally got a view of what made Bristol Bay the most legendary salmon fishery in the world. At slack water the river was absolutely alive with jumping fish— easily 100 fish were in the air at once, stretching out as far as our eyes could see! From the radio reports the other rivers were experiencing similar abundance. This was the 'peak' that might be gone in only a few days. The fish in front us were waiting for the tide to take advantage of the added push— although another day we would see them buck the strong current in their eagerness to complete the long journey home. Many would be allowed through for the health of future generations.

In twenty minutes the 12-hour period would open, but now the second starter wouldn't kick the motor over. I glanced over the gunnel at the splashes in the water, knowing perhaps 20% of our season rested on our success in the next few hours.

"Goddamnit to hell you worthless, rusty, lubbering piece of flotsam!" I yelled, desperately whacking it with violent hammer blows in an attempt to get it to do its job.

The persuasion finally worked. With huge relief we motored out and started jockeying for a good starting position. We were near the beach with many of the other 400 boats fishing the area. The area would soon be laced with a thick gauntlet of nets, but there would be enough for everyone.

We were looking for a good concentration of fish, but didn't want to 'cork' anyone. Corking someone, we had discovered, is a bad thing. It means you have put your net too close in front of theirs and are rudely stealing their fish.

At the exact opening time we slowly eased the net out towards the shore, giving plenty of room to our neighbors. A high-powered, fiberglass boat waited nearby for half our set. Mimicking the consideration a killer whale gives to wounded prey, he laid his net in front of ours, corking us badly. It was the smirk on his face that bothered me most.

Shar dropped the buoy and I turned hard left to drive back to the other end. Abruptly, the steering wheel fell off and landed on the deck in three pieces! *Rebel*, stuck hard over and going full-throttle, did a wide circle around the corking culprit. We crossed over his set, leaving skewed line and bits of cork in our wake. Failing to make contact with our gear that time around, we started another circle. As we cut his net again, I tried, through gesticulations and smiles, to indicate the innocence of our maneuvers. But, from his answering gestures and jumping about, I was not communicating well enough.

Continuing the circle, we crossed his net a third time and were able to finally hook ours at the moment the engine died. I ducked my head into the engine compartment and yelled back, "The fuel filter is full of water! I'll empty it while you try to pull the net in."

After draining the water the boat coughed and finally started. We hauled the net full of thrashing fish into the stern and, following a number of carefully timed pirouettes, managed to drop the anchor in relative safety along the shore before the engine died again. I knew we were doomed with all the water that must be in the bad fuel we had pumped into the tank. Another tow was our only option. The fleet, however, was loading up with fresh sockeye, and help was not coming soon.

Instead, the wind came, increasing to 35 knots during the next hour. *Rebel* was rearing in the surf against the anchor like a wild animal. At last our dilemma ended in a heart-pounding rescue. I had to cut the anchor-line before we could be dragged out—wallowing with hundreds of gallons of shipped water in the bilge. Shar remained steadfast in the stern, picking fish from the piled high net, while heaving her previously consumed breakfast over the side between fish.

•

Back on the beach I drained the water from the fuel, lashed a stick onto the steering wheel stub, replaced some missing bolts on the flapping rudder, and pounded some more caulk into the seams. Armed with a new anchor, we pushed *Rebel* back in at low tide and anchored off Coffee Point. The same gale winds resumed with the rising tide. The washing machine effect kicked in quickly. It was imperative we leave immediately!

In quick discussion with Shar I said, "I don't like you on the bow one bit, but with all the tricks *Rebel* is capable of, I think I should drive...it's the best of a bad situation."

"I think you're right. Hand me that lifejacket."

"Don't forget, one hand for yourself, one for the ship."

She crawled forward and wasn't in position more than a few seconds when the wicked waves breaking over the bow buried her. Following her shouted request for slack, she at last cleared the anchor from the bottom. Somehow, in her own desperation, she stuck the flukes into the rotted wooden hull.

"I'll take her around the point." I bellowed into the wind.

"Anywhere but here." I think she yelled back.

Faced with my bad anchoring decision, the dangerous extraction, and the *Rebel*—I went momentarily insane. As soon as we reached the relative shelter around the point, I kicked the anchor free and, expelling long pent-up rage, jerked it out of the water so hard it arched overhead and crashed on the foredeck of a boat we had drifted near, nearly smashing his windshield. I calmed down enough to make the necessary apologies, and we pulled away to grab a soggy few hours rest. Pounding rain arrived with the wind and flowed freely through the deck onto our sleeping bags.

•

The awful sound of tortured machinery pierced the strangely quiet morning when I attempted to start-up. The sticky starter had reversed its ailments and now would not disengage after the motor was running. Grabbing the nearby wrench, I loosened the bolts and jerked the housing off the engine to free it.

Back in the game, the day stayed fair as we set the net and started catching good fish on our drift towards the north end of the district. After estimating our position, I turned and saw the bottom of a pair of frantically kicking boots sticking above the outside of the roller. Investigating the odd scene, I found Shar upside down in the net, stretched over the water as if in a frozen dive. Her hands were locked into the gills of a huge king salmon that must have topped 50 pounds

"Hold on," I encouraged, "I'll get the gaff!"

"Be careful with that thing!" I heard her gasp, a touch of fear tainting her voice. She knew my theory of gaffing was: *if you don't sink the iron, you at least should stun the fish with the blow.*

14

"You're a heroine and you'll have my best effort!" I called as I rushed forward.

I grabbed the evil hooked weapon from the cuddy and ran back aft, winding up like a javelin thrower, blindly flailing it over the transom and striking hard.

Shar called me crazy, and the between-the-eyes strike, luck. I, of course, called it skill. There was great joy in having them both aboard.

That night the king was the last fish we sold to the buying tender. We were heading for the mooring when the engine emitted a loud, relinquishing burp. This was followed by a horrible clanking noise. Dense smoke belched from the stack. The pea-soup appearance of the oil meant salt water had made its way inside. This indicated severe internal injury. Pronounced DOA, *Rebel* was granted the death certificate she had so fervently been seeking.

I looked at Shar, "Well, I guess *Rebel* won. I don't think we made enough to pay the bills. Looks like I'll be crabbing in the Bering Sea this winter for sure. It's interesting how fighting this ongoing disaster has become normal."

She smiled gamely and said, "We'll be back, and we'll be happy knowing it can't get any worse than this. Besides, being offered the helping hands of so many people has been a true heart-opening experience. It's been worth it for that alone."

•

Nine months later I was walking on the Egegik beach when I spotted a familiar blue color along the bank: yes! I recognized my bow patch. It was surely the *Rebel*, flat as a flounder, as close to the ground as she could get. I sensed she was happy serving another incarnation preventing erosion.

In a weirdly paradoxical way we had served each other well and, in the end, each found ourselves just where we wanted to be. I had learned a lot in a short period from *Rebel*, and noted there were no hard feelings. I threw an old tire over her, anchoring the pieces more securely, and walked towards the new season ahead.

CHAPTER 2

RAMMED

≈

The "call to adventure"...transferred his spiritual center of gravity from within the pale of his society to a zone unknown. This fateful region of both treasure and danger may be variously represented...but it is always a place of strangely fluid and polymorphous beings, unimaginable torments, superhuman deeds, and impossible delight.

—Joseph Campbell,
The Hero with a Thousand faces

The shingles and tarpaper were gone in an instant, ripped away as surely as a page torn in anger from this book. The wind intensified as it funneled through the mountains, assaulting the small house with blasts over 100 miles-per-hour. Next, the brutal barrage started in on the roof boards themselves, tearing five or six off, each instantly following the other. The yanked nails screeched like tortured cats before the boards launched somewhere far off into the freezing, black Alaskan night.

This was the second winter storm packing hurricane winds I had experienced since flying into Dutch Harbor, Alaska (some 600 miles westerly down the Aleutian chain, and nearly equidistant from Seattle, Hawaii and Japan). I made the trip to hustle-up a job on one of the big steel boats hunting king crab in the infamous Bering Sea.

17

I wanted this job for a number of reasons: Our first salmon season in Bristol Bay had been more rich with learning experiences than money; I also was seeking personal vindication for a bad decision I had made two years before. I had trusted a man from Anchorage named Tom Williams with the money my wife, Shar, and I had saved for a Bristol Bay limited entry permit. He owned the permit and signed it over to us, but lost it to his partner in a dispute before the transfer occurred. He spent our money and had no assets for us to attach in recovering the loss. I had absorbed the important part of the lesson: the futility of revenge and its detrimental effects on me as 'victim' (or, said another way, realizing that laying awake night after night cutting William's heart out with a dull knife was doing me much more harm than him). The money was the bulk of our savings. In Dutch, I wanted to tangibly correct my mistake and make back the money I felt so bad about losing. The fact that I was young, strong, seeking extreme adventure on the edge, and keen on discovering more about myself, only complemented the moral mission.

•

I listened to the storm relentlessly whip the harbor just below and wondered how much more of the old house was going to give itself up to the omnipotent force of the storm. I moved into the small abandoned structure when I first arrived. I assumed the house, attractively perched on a hill above the harbor, was some officers' quarters left over from the significant military presence established in Dutch Harbor during W.W.II. Protecting myself against a few leaks, I set up my tent inside, a home within a home, and turned it back into an appreciated shelter. At the time, this seemed like the better alternative to camping in the open somewhere, or living like a hedgehog in one of the carved-out caves honeycombing the island. Right now, with the entire structure creaking in agony and threatening to do a Wizard-of-Oz lift-off, I thought the cave dweller existence I had rejected now seemed like a fine idea. But hadn't this thing withstood Bering Sea winters for thirty-seven years? Apparently its number was up. The next cycle of ferocious blasts claimed another eight feet of roof boards, tearing them away with the rapidity—and sweaty accompanying fear—of machine gun fire. I was sure I was headed for Kansas.

•

Dutch Harbor, indisputably one of the most savaged places on earth in the dead of winter, was the busiest landing port for the lucrative Alaskan king crab industry. It was also Club Med. to the fifty bald eagles I counted one fall evening perched on every point commanding any view of the surroundings. The giant crab made big money for those with the vessels that could withstand the beatings the Bering Sea consistently delivered. When the boats cleared the protection of Dutch, outbound to challenge the Bering Sea and try to wrest its bounty from her depths, only the strong survived. Few knew in November of 1977 the end of the king crab boom was peeking over the horizon; but this year the best skippers, the highliners, would put in over a million pounds in three months! Full crew shares averaged 8% after expenses, and $75,000-plus for the three-month season was not crazy talk.

•

The house vibrated with another fierce onslaught of compressed air. I crouched over like a sprinter in the starting blocks, a few essentials stuffed in my backpack, ready to run for it. My senses were tuned to high intensity flight mode. There was flying sheet metal out there, scything through the air looking to cut something down. Bolting for the caves was a last card I did not want to play.

Nothing tore off during the hit. That last blast turned out to be the moment the storm started abating. In the dark dawn hours I finally fell asleep, confident I would wake in the same place.

•

My strategy was to get up early to be the first on deck of the newly arrived boats. I would find them delivering their loads to the numerous processors ringing the harbor. The alternative

19

was to hangout late in the notorious Elbow Room bar and network with the crews, but I could not possibly keep that insane, hung-over pace and accomplish anything during the day.

I was up later than usual the morning after the storm. I made my normal rounds of the harbor ferreting out any vacancies. This included visiting with a growing list of acquaintances as their boats cycled in to unload every week or two, depending on their fishing success. This was the varsity team, and any crewman making it as far as the Bering Sea king crab fishery knew what they were getting into. They tended to hold fast to the opportunity. Most open spots came about due to injury or a serious personality conflict. Luckily, I wasn't 'green', having previous experience crabbing in Cook Inlet. Still, I had already passed on a few offers from boats with pirate reputations, heavy drug use, or maniacal skippers. But the turnover was slow on the good boats—and I was not the only one looking for a job. With big money involved, it was interesting to see how the crews rallied to the common cause and invented ways to work together.

Though the men (and a few women) working these boats had faired well economically during the boom years, other costs were extremely high. Sinkings, injury and drowings were uncomfortably common in the Bering Sea, subsequently earning commercial fishing the dubious number one spot as the deadliest job in the world. At its worst time, an average of one fisherman was killed each week!

The boats, generally 90-to-160 feet long, were tough-ass, handsome warriors of the sea. Built of steel for the incredible stresses the North Pacific was capable of delivering, even the biggest and toughest were frequently handed lessons in humility.

The afternoon after the storm, I talked to one crewman on his panicked rush to the airport. His face was cut and bruised. Reflected in his eyes was the raw vulnerability and stark intensity from having experienced his life nearly snuffed out in an instant—without anyone knowing what had happened. The night my shelter was being torn apart, his boat was running for protection in the maw of the same storm. His voice quivered with emotion as he told his story:

"It was blowin' ninety miles-an-hour and gettin' stronger. I had the early morning shift. At about 02:00 I was watchin' what had to be goddamn fifty-foot waves come into the range of the crab lights and roll right down on us. We were ridin' up and over them pretty good, but still there was plenty of water hittin' the windows and flyin' over the top. We were startin' to make ice on the railing. I'm pressin' my face against the glass, lookin' ahead with my hand sweatin' on the throttle, ready to back her down."

He looked down for a moment, slowly shaking his head at the memory. I thought he might breakdown and seemed to welcome my hand on his shoulder. He continued after a long moment.

"Suddenly the window next to my head exploded...like a bomb hit it or somethin', and I'm punched out of the chair and smashed on the deck by a cold fist of water and glass! I never saw the rogue bastard come out of the dark before it knocked us hard over on our ear. It didn't stop there! Before I could figure out what the hell happened, it washed me down the stairs and left me beat-to-shit on the galley floor. I can't *believe* we made it in! This sure as hell is not worth my life!" Then he was gone, running towards the sanctuary of his plane.

I went down to look at his boat. She was a stout, house-forward, 108-footer. The builder was known for seaworthy vessels. The invading rogue wave had broken out a number of pilothouse windows, still haphazardly covered with plywood. The water drowned many of the electronics in the wheelhouse. Breaking welds and shearing bolts, the impact of the knockout punch had torqued the entire wheelhouse six inches out of alignment. Her hunting was over for the season.

Late in the afternoon I selected yet another book from the library, settled down at the mouth of the harbor and waited like a raptor for new prey; I was loaded with patience and purpose.

•

Early in November, six weeks pounding the docks finally landed me a job on the *Sea Venture*. She was a reputable house-forward, 104-foot crabber built by MARCO, a quality shipyard in Seattle known for building handsome, rugged boats for the Bering Sea. Spreading my bag out on my new berth, I was enthusiastic about leaving and optimistic, along with my three veteran deckmates, that the good fishing would continue with half the season still ahead.

We cleared Dutch, left Priest Rock on the starboard side like so many eager predators before, and started rolling with the Bering Sea swells. It was a new world of humming machinery and motion with little connecting it to the weathered land receding behind.

We had a thirty-six hour run to the gear that was left soaking during the last delivery. When called for my turn at the wheel, I made my way to the bridge. I was determined to show Kris, the captain, my seamanlike abilities and gung-ho attitude.

While he explained my duties and gave me the course to steer, I struggled mightily to appear cool and professional. Finally, abandoning all effort, I abruptly left him mid-sentence and lurched out the cabin door to puke my guts over the railing into the sea. There was no point explaining I had never been on a fishing boat longer than sixty-feet and was, until then, unconscious of what real seasickness felt like. I was discovering the full extent of this horrible affliction in the slower righting motion of the bigger boat running in fifteen-foot seas. He was even less impressed with me when I had to wake him up mid-watch to repeat the course I was to steer. I had forgotten it after turning off the autopilot to dodge crab buoys. When my watch ended, I staggered below and collapsed in my bunk, wishing for a knock on the head that might induce a short-term coma, hoping I might somehow recover before I was needed on deck. Not a chance!

The dreaded call to start hauling gear finally came. Before we went out Kris sketched the situation: The polar icepack was drifting south, we were near its edge and had to pull and stack our pots before they were carried away, or broken off by the ice. *Great,* I thought, *we get to start off sprinting!*

I donned my oilskins over heavy under layers of wool and synthetic clothes. My hood was up and cinched when the Doug, the first mate, handed me four thick rubber bands—the unique symbol of a Bering Sea crabber. He said, "You'll need these around your pant cuffs when the water goes above your boots."

The shocking ice-cold reality of the Bering Sea hit me in the face the instant I stepped out the watertight door to the back deck. Beyond the sodium deck lights it was as black as the inside of a nun's habit. Appearing from the darkness, snow and spray shot sideways across the rails, pushed by a strong fifty-knot wind. I couldn't help marveling at the beautiful rime of ice covering everything but the ironwood deck planks themselves—a fairyland in the middle of hell! The boat heaved, struggling to dump the foot of freezing water that had just poured over the rail, burying the deck. At seven degrees below freezing, it looked and felt completely inhospitable and alien.

The four of us started hauling fast! The routine kicked in easily: grappling buoys, coiling 50-to-90 fathoms (300-to-540-feet) of line as it dumped off the power block, hooking and lifting the huge 7'X7' pot—which exceeded 1000 pounds with any crab inside—over the railing onto the launching rack, and emptying it before dragging it aft with the boom hook to join the growing load. I eventually found a bizarre place of sanctuary: twenty-one feet atop the swaying three-tiered stack, chaining the pots to the boat with binders. Clinging to the web, and solitude, of this wild loft, I could dry-heave in my private misery—dignity, or image be damned. Back on deck I eyed the hydraulic bait chopper: an evil machine, the one that reduced a forty-pound block of frozen herring to confetti in an instant. For one second that first night I contemplated putting my hand in and hope for a light wound. The evacuation would have provided temporary relief, but I determined I would have to put my head in for the relief I sought.

●

My appetite and strength returned on the third day at sea. By then I was well used to the flow of the deck. We would rotate positions throughout the short day and long night—darkness prevailed in the eighteen hours after sunset (were we to ever see one) as we approached the winter solstice, a month away. The only sleep we snatched as brief catnaps, frequently flopped on the galley floor in full raingear while we ran to another string of pots.

We ran south and dumped the 150 pots rescued from the advancing icepack in an area on the chart called, the 'Slime Banks'. This move developed into a classic yin/yang situation of good and suffering rolled into one. On one hand the crab were plentiful, arriving at the surface averaging forty big 'keepers' to a pot, with few undersized ones to sort and throw back. That was the good part. The downside became evident when the first buoy was grappled and I started coiling the 60 fathoms (360-feet) of three-quarter-inch line pinched in the sheave of the hydraulic hauling block. The line feeding off suddenly metamorphosed into a slippery living thing. Glancing over the rail, I saw the line come out of water as thick as my wrist, appearing like a freshly dissected artery, gooped with slimy red, stinging jellyfish. The ladened rope hit the constricting sheave, wringing off the bulk of the mess, which either plopped back into the water in bucket loads or flew off the block and coated the deck as if some disgusting Hollywood monster had exploded over us. Tucking my head as deeply into my hood as I could, I concentrated on my job while the poisonous tentacles steadily rained on my back and finally began dripping past my face like snot. The pot finally broke the surface, unrecognizable with red goo coating every inch of web and steel. The rigging above groaned and snapped with the additional weight when we hauled it over the rail.

More groans and yelps then usual were added to the usual sounds on deck during our five days hauling and setting on the Slime Bank. When someone caught a tentacle on his cheek, it felt like a lash from red-hot barbed wire, and needed to be scrapped off immediately. The worse cursing came when someone caught one in the eye, necessitating a headlong lurch into the galley for copious amounts of freshwater rinsing.

•

The days rolled together. My hands were swollen, unaccustomed to pushing pots around, changing bait, and coiling untold miles of line each day. Any rest over an hour and they would become numb—useless until shaken and beat into usefulness again.

I began to understand the myriad ways one could be maimed or killed while crabbing.   Of course, the vessel itself was the first defense against the sea and weather, which never seemed to blow less than twenty-five knots, and usually over thirty-five. The dangerous mix came with the great weight of a deck load of pots (70,000 pounds on our vessel) stacked above the waterline, 50,000 gallons of diesel fuel sloshing around in tanks below deck, swimming pool-sized crab tanks full of water, some inexperienced crews, and icing conditions, all contributed to a frightening amount of boats lost due to rollover.   Technology and regulation finally improved the dismal safety record substantially, but the danger was especially stark in these earlier years.

Out on the slippery, rolling deck there were numerous opportunities to crush body parts.   Severed fingers were very common.   Too many times, in response to shouts of danger lurking near, I hit the deck in a reflexive survival ball.   A renegade pot hoisted over the rail could cut a wild wrecking ball swath over the deck before it was dropped into the pot launcher.   Pots lined up for stacking would sometimes break loose across the tilting deck, or lurch enough to buck anyone on top off into the water.   I was cautioned early on to be particularly alert when reaching in and pulling out crab or changing bait; everyone had a story of someone going over in a pot when the boat took a severe roll, trapped and plummeting to the bottom like a cannonball.   Additionally, being swept off ones' feet by a boarding wave and dumped flailing into the scuppers was a constant threat.   But the PRIMARY problem compounding all the danger, was the numbing, repetitious work and ever-present fatigue that dulled the senses when they should have been on full, 'RED ALERT!

•

I was stunned at the amount of crab we sometimes set our pots on.   Not infrequently they would come up with crushed crab on the outside of the bottom webbing, indicating the pot had landed on a thick field of king crab below. The web, bulging with healthy crab on the inside, confirmed the population density.   It was fishing the dream during those times and everyone grinned like fools.

We delivered another 100,000 pounds in Dutch early December. Being the new guy, I volunteered to watch the boat while the rest hit town during the short turn-around. I did manage to get to a phone and tell Shar not to sell my stuff, that I had made some dough, and expected to arrive home with more by Christmas.

Early evening, five days into our new trip, Kris came out of the wheelhouse and informed us of the storm bearing down on us. It was, without a doubt, going to be a big league Beaufort Force 12, maximum intensity storm. We would need to quickly move gear still farther south, or risk losing it to the encroaching icepack. Then, with no time to run for cover, we would ride out the storm at sea.

The edge was sharpening, tension building, as we scrambled for the next sixteen hours. The wind pressure increased against our hunched shoulders with each passing hour—the long tentacles of the unseen monster reaching over the horizon and announcing its imminent arrival. Great volumes of dark water poured over the railing on the rolls. The wind was blowing sixty knots when we dumped the last pot and lashed everything down. What, I wondered, were the live crab in the flooded tanks thinking as the turbulence increased? Maybe something along the lines with us: How much worse will this get, and where would we be in twenty-four hours?

It was hunker-down time. Those not on watch wedged into our bunks using any spare padding. We tried not to think about the cold and building ferocity inches away on the other side of the steel hull. The angle of roll and pitch increased hourly. I dozed fitfully, frequently going airborne before abruptly plopping back to the mattress. The engine speed was set just enough to maintain position while we jogged into the building seas. We would pitch up radically as we climbed the steepening waves, shuddering at the top when the bow slammed through the breaking crest. Next, we would pivot abruptly over the lip, the engine racing for an instant as the propeller spun in the air, before the boat plunged precipitously down the backside. Accelerating down the wave, we would nose deeply into the trough, producing a deep vibration tremor that resonated throughout the vessel.

Summoned for my watch, I rolled out and found the motion so extreme that crawling on hands and knees was safer and more expedient than walking. The boat felt alive and stressed. Creeping past the galley, I tucked a rolling can of tuna fish into my vest as I inched by. I glanced at the refrigerator, hoping the bolts securing it to the deck were stout. There were great forces urging it to leap from its alcove and fall across the cabin on one of our deep rolls. Opening the heavy door leading aft, I realized I had been getting only the PG-rating, the toned down version lying in my bunk. There was far more water than deck showing. The temperature was a numbing twenty-degrees Fahrenheit—the chill factor must have been on the end of the scale. Looking towards the stern, the thwartship bulwarks angled steeply away from what I thought was the horizon; the port and starboard ice-sheathed railings appeared like fences protruding from deep winter snow. They stuck up lonely above the broiling whitewater pouring off the planks buried beneath. Pulling the can of tuna out of my pocket, I chucked it high over the side and saw it snatched sideways by the blast, carried away astern, never touching the water.

Gaining the bridge, I gawked at the sea, white and in a raging fury of spray filled, tumultuous chaos. The wind was roaring like a jet, a steady 100 mph! Higher gusts ripped the tops off the advancing seas, filling the air like shards of glass and lashing us with their watery shattered remains. The bigger waves topped fifty feet—I suspect somewhat curtailed in size by the relatively short fetch of the land forty miles in front of us. Though repeatedly staggered, the boat still seemed to be able to efficiently shake off the tremendous weight of solid water crashing on the bow as she plowed into the valleys. With this shaky confidence, I was more awestruck than frightened.

The main waves came in the predictable general rhythm of an attacking army. But there were often unpredictable smaller waves, like recreant foot soldiers appearing to either side, striking us jarring blows without warning. Eerily, when we dove down the backside of a large sea, the deafening sound outside would quiet considerably. Looking up at the roofless room of water around us, the boat I once imagined as so big, now felt incredibly small.

We faced a dire concern as the storm raged into the second day. The slow build-up of ice we were watching on the railing was approaching the size of a mans thigh. *Sea Venture's* motion was becoming increasingly sluggish. Between waves, a furtive glance out the door up at the high rigging confirmed the antennas and mast starting to look like winterized, ice encased high altitude conifers. The added weight of tons of ice settled the boat deeper in the water and slowed her recovery. We were taking more frequent trembling hits of solid water that threatened to smash the windows. The sea state remained in a wild frenzy of flying spindrift, mixed in a cacophony of howling wind, and showed no sighs of abating. A short while later first one, then the other radar froze. This surely marked the start of our slide over the thin edge we had been riding as mere battered passengers, into a must-take-action survival mode.

The mission was clear: We had to chop the ice away from the superstructure to reduce the weight aloft and allow the boat to better defend herself from the onslaught. The thought of going out on deck in these conditions chilled us all to the core. I thought of the panicked Dutch Harbor survivor and better understood his rushed retreat to the airport.

We assembled below, garbed in every insulating piece of clothing we could find, cuffs and wrists tightly taped, safety lines binding our waists and each clutching a baseball bat, ax or hammer—strange gladiators bound for some savage game without rules.

Adding a full burst of power to the engine, Kris spun the boat in a well-timed maneuver to turn and run with the smoking tempest. We crept out, clutching anything solid with a death-grip. It was slow going. We eventually spread out at our assigned positions. It was impossible exposing even a little facial skin to the wind for more than a moment—the pelting spray was too painful and it was difficult to breathe. With our backs to the onslaught, we tied off and—more than sufficiently charged with fear—started swinging like madmen at the ice encrusting the boat. Staggering around trying to maintain balance and launch effective blows at the ice, we must have appeared like rioting drunks on a rampage.

After four hours of frantic whacking, *Sea Venture* finally responded to our efforts. Her roll was livelier and she seemed lighter afoot. We gratefully re-entered the warmth of the ship with a revived sense of confidence regarding our survival.

The lifting shroud of dawn signaled the third day. The wind started to diminish steadily and by 10:00 we were back at work. The storm lingered as a humbling memory, eliciting renewed respect for nature and individual metaphysical reflections on life. In my own thankful state, between the violent storm and peaceful dawn, I felt blissfully balanced and closely connected to a benevolent Spirit.

•

Mere days after the storm, we arrived at a new string of pots and arose from our brief rest to view the sunrise illuminating a rare calm, placid sea. The sun brought a wonderful warm gentle wind with it. In celebration we prepared a huge breakfast. Inspecting the radar, we saw nothing within ten miles of us, and all sat down to an uncommon moment of group relaxation, leaving the boat to drift on the flat ocean. Everyone felt the season winding down, the end well in sight. Though dead-in-the-water, but technically underway, it seemed unnecessary to keep a man constantly on watch in light of such a quiet morning, so we checked the radar again before the second helpings were served, noticing only a lone vessel on the horizon. The mood was as light as the day and the meal stretched on, everyone loath to disturb the peacefulness.

Suddenly, a tremendous crash echoed through the hull, followed by an unbelievable force violently slamming the boat over onto its side! At the same instant the generators died, pitching the galley into near darkness. From the lone light emitting through the porthole, I could see bodies and cutlery flying across the cabin and thudding into the bulkhead on the opposite side. We each fully expected the rush of freezing water to burst over us and inundate the cabin, trapping us in a steel tomb to lie forever on the ocean bottom as many had before us. Miraculously, after a long frozen moment, *Sea Venture* started to roll back upright. I struggled to my feet trying to regain my bearings. Feeling no icy water, I dashed out the door. Behind

29

me, I heard the tense, desperate voices of two crewmen arguing over a survival suit clutched between them.

On deck I grabbed a coil of line and climbed to the bridge level. Spotting the *Amatuli* nearby, a 114-foot, house-aft black crabber with a full load of pots, the picture became clearer. She was dead-in-the-water and sported a crushed bow. While Kris and Doug checked the inside of the boat, I rigged a line and repelled over the starboard rail, just forward of the house. The hull was holed and badly caved in, but the damage was above the waterline and we were not taking on any water. The impact of the blow, it appeared, had been slightly angled forward and, though rolling us severely, had allowed the *Amatuli* to grind by. A deep chill buzzed up my spine realizing that, had we been T-boned squarely, the tremendous weight and momentum of the heavy crabber would probably have continued over the top of us and sunk the boat!

The shocks were not over. Going below I walked into our stateroom amid chaos. Mattresses, clothes and splintered wood were everywhere. The impact had hit my upper bunk dead center—the bunk I had left an hour before—destroying it entirely.

The degree of responsibility we needed to take (for not keeping a continuous watch) did little to quell my seething anger when I heard of the unforgivable offense committed aboard our attacker: A crewman had fallen asleep at the wheel and effectively turned the loaded ship into an unguided missile of potential destruction—and manslaughter. I took it personally and desperately wanted to go aboard and beat the culprit bloody for his crime. Endangering my own life by choice was one thing; having someone else threaten my mates and me with an act of irresponsible idiocy when our backs were turned, sparked in me raw indignation and a need for immediate, God-like retribution. But the boats remained drifting apart. Insufficient apologizes were made over the radio. I would have to be satisfied with the karmic justice the irresponsible driver would eventually receive.

104′ *Sea Venture* ready to hunt king crab in the Bering Sea.

The long tentacles of the approaching storm reach out

Amatuli—dressed for summer

Our season was over! Seattle was the only place to safely access the potential unseen damage and make repairs. Still stunned from the sudden turn of events, we turned and cautiously steamed for Dutch. There the shaft was checked for alignment and the operating systems tested. A temporary patch covered the pierced hull while arrangements were made for another boat to care for our pots. In a few days we castoff the lines for the ten day run to Seattle. Adding an appreciated degree of comfort, we ran in company with another vessel also seeking the TLC the city had to offer.

The voyage was a slow time of watches, eating, reading and reflection. I appreciated the experiences winter crabbing in the Bering Sea had brought. I made exactly the amount of money I had lost in the permit fiasco. For me, *and* my marriage, I felt with so many close calls it would be foolish to tempt fate again.

As I drove east with a box of Christmas king crab strapped to the bumper, I recognized my purpose lay in other pursuits, including making my own salmon and herring fisheries' in Bristol Bay all they could be. I would fish halibut in the Bering Sea during a different season, but I would not crab again. It had been a wild ride indeed, but I would leave the Bering Sea winter to other intrepid seamen and their various reasons for being there. They alone would face the very real rewards, and failures, it had waiting for them.

CHAPTER 3

THE SINKING OF THE *WHITE DAWN*

≈

> Only to the extent that man exposes himself to annihilation can that which is indestructible arise within him. In this lies the dignity of daring.

—Karlfried Graf Durkheim

We flew away from the suicidal *Rebel* after the 1977 season feeling wave-rolled and beach slammed. We were also pretty much broke. Yet, in the aftermath of the experience, we felt infused with a life-affirming afterglow having survived and realized the potential of making a few dollars in the process. One thing was abundantly clear: we needed a boat of our own.

That winter, the money I made crabbing in the Bering Sea went towards catch-up expenses. We were trying to live a beer lifestyle on a lemonade budget, deciding what to do about a boat for the next season. I called Bill De Rosier, boss of the cannery we fished for, and inquired what was for sale in Naknek. He described the classic beauty and reliability of an old wooden bowpicker sitting two thousand miles away on his dock. But there were two looming and vitally more important facts that finally convinced me to buy her over the phone: she came cheap, <u>and</u> on credit.

•

The next spring my heart was immediately touched by her grace the moment I saw the bowpicker perched on the dock in

Naknek. Surrounded by fancy fiberglass sternpickers—and shortly before the birth of the behemoth aluminum boat generation—she looked to me like a lovely wallflower patiently waiting for some brave soul to ask her to dance. I saw beyond the strange plywood hump on her back (an Alaskan addition); I was the smitten guy. Honoring a new chapter for us in the far north, I named her *White Dawn*.

She was a thirty-two foot Columbia River bowpicker, an elegant survivor from the days after 1950 when motors were finally allowed in Bristol Bay. She arrived soon after the last canvas sail was furled on the spritsail rigged, double-ended sailboats—the durable workhorses that netted sockeye and sailed those waters for over half a century. Immediately following the liberation, a potpourri fleet of different motorized boats from 'outside' was shipped north to take the place of sail. It was hoped the bowpickers, although designed for the lighter salmon fishing found on the great Columbian artery, would meet the demands of a new era of doing business in Bristol Bay.

White Dawn carried the graceful, well-proportioned soft lines of a properly built wooden boat. The fine arching stem gently puffed into the sensuous curves defined by the yellow cedar planking that swathed her steamed oak ribs. From there the seams swept aft along a perfect sheer line to the unobtrusive rounded trunk of the cabin.

The sexiness ended there. In adapting to the nastier Alaskan weather, a horribly ugly, tall plywood box had been added to extend the cabin aft and enclose the original exposed steering station in the stern cockpit. It was referred to as 'the outhouse'. In fairness, it did serve its functional purpose of offering shelter and a place to contemplate a lashing storm, or the shifting neighborhood on a long night drift.

Even farther back was another addition unique to Bristol Bay: ramming protection. Hanging over the water, behind the hard lines of the outhouse, was a heavy steel horizontal bar arching out from each corner of the stern, resembling the faceguard on a football helmet. Two diagonal legs—welded to the outside of the halo and bolted to the bottom plank of the transom—held up this deadweight. I always thought the armor contrasted harshly with the grace of her lines. It made the boat look ridiculously like a gowned woman who, having been bound for the ball, had gotten terribly lost and ended up in the gladiator arena with a shield hastily attached to her arm— neither fit the other. That disconnected vision portended the ironic fact the armor would be the chink that would almost end *White Dawn's* days forever.

•

The plan was for Shar to fish with me early for kings, and again later for silvers and pink salmon. Mid-season she would learn the setnetting game on the beach, building experience toward a planned future of fishing with small children. I hated to lose her—easily one of the best crewmates I would ever work with. As an example, later that season, on our six-hour night run to reported good humpy fishing in the Nushagak, I watched her tuck herself into the spray drenched bow of the *White Dawn* and hang new web on the corkline <u>and</u> leadline of the net we would fish the next day...impressive by any standards!

Her good-natured personality and blue eyes earned her endless help and tips from the venerable Italian contingent at the cannery—and we needed it. Their hundreds of combined years of rich experience flowed our way, weaving its way through net hanging theory, fishing counsel, and how to keep the engine in the *White Dawn* running flawlessly.

•

It must be said that Shar did not always have her way. One recent winter we were living in a rustic cabin across Kachemak Bay from Homer, Alaska. She had chicken parts laid out on the counter preparing for dinner. Out of the corner of her eye she saw a leg start to slide away toward the shadows. Reaching over to grab one end, she found a feisty white ermine on the other end, his black tipped tail whipping the air in all the excitement. They tugged back and forth for a while, first one gaining ground, then the other, Shar scolding the bandit all the while for his audacity. In a flash of brilliance, she reached over, picked up the peppershaker and shook it over his snout. The sneezing retreat of the weasel was not pretty, nor was the wounded look he gave her before scampering off to his hidden sanctuary. The woman was rather pleased with the victory until we went to bed later that night. Smack in the middle of her pillow was a neat puddle of ermine pepper puke.

•

Belying her outward grace, Spartan would not be off the mark in describing the interior of our new boat. Still, it was a substantial step-up from the *Rebel.* Sticking up in the center of the 'outhouse' was a five-foot length of pipe. This was the gearshift. It connected to the naked iron of the Chrysler Crown, flathead engine sitting in the middle of the main cabin, two steps down from the outhouse. Bolted to the top of this classic was a table physically linking the two bunks on either side for the common purpose of sharing food or playing cards. Care had to be taken to avoid knocking the ignition coil with a knee or, alternatively, burning a leg on the engine housing.

The noise was deafening when the six flashing cylinders reached peak RPM. Tissue paper in our ears was poor protection from the din. Yet oddly, sleeping two feet away from that screaming hot steel afforded some of the soundest sleep I ever experienced.

The state of our electronics was pitiful. We had upgraded to two radios in the cabin. Along with the CB, we now had a VHF. But I could not get away from the Bristol Bay sailboat oar I had grown accustomed to using as a depth finder on the *Rebel.* It did, however, afford me some comfort in the twisted delusion that I could row the boat somewhere if the engine were to quit. Life seemed simple and good.

•

Charlie McCrum, Shar's brother-in-law, had enough adventurous spirit to join me for the main sockeye run. He was a hard-working, easygoing fellow who, most importantly, was stronger than I in the mechanical field.

We worked hard and were well cared for by the cannery with offered warm bunks ashore and three hearty meals per day, along with two mug-ups.

Early in June we somewhat reluctantly unsuckled from the mother cannery's teat and headed *White Dawn* down the river. We would not be returning for five weeks.

New stacked nets surrounded our small world. Mixed-in was the smell of fresh paint and freshly oiled machinery. We were bound thirty-five miles south for the familiar territory of the Egegik district, eager to match our eager energy with that of the first returning wild salmon. Money aside, I felt both the fish and us drawing ever towards each other, driven by individually programmed instincts.

We arrived on the grounds, fueled up, off- loaded our spare nets and started fishing. I quickly resumed the slow climb up the learning curve I'd started the past season. There were evidently still more unexplored sandbars to run aground on and, as I pushed the edges, innumerable ways to blunder and feel like an idiot.

The new boat allowed us—along with a blazing eight knots of speed—much greater range of the district than the *Rebel* had permitted. Sometimes the range was too great. One morning, after pushing ourselves ridiculously hard for four days and few fish, I was jolted from an exhausted sleep on the outhouse bench by the cacophony of loud rapping on the deck. Dan Veerhusen, a friend and fellow old-boat-owner, had sympathetically run outside the district boundaries to find us on the horizon. He told me that while I might be pleased with the one shackle of net hanging off our bow, even more impressive were the other two I had left behind when our net broke in half wrapping a processor ship anchored at the legal boundary line, *a mile back*! This kind of careless fishing would not be brooked in future years when 100-feet over the line would cost $3000, or forfeiture of a season.

•

Another cycle of the greatest sockeye salmon migration on the planet arrived with a frenetic punch early in July. Early on Fish and Game mandated downtime, allowing 'windows' for escapement and the health of future generations. We might fish for 16-hours, deliver, and raft-up to socialize with friends at midnight over a glass of wine in the inviting cabin of a friend. It seemed the tensions of the day were in direct proportion to the camaraderie and relaxation of the evening.

The fish poured under us in ever-greater numbers until we had to start stopping them to prevent over-escapement. We started fishing under full steam on July 6.

●

Early Bristol Bay sailboats getting towed out for a week of fishing. Some of these were motorized in 1951. (photo courtesy of National Maritime Museum, San Francisco)

The author aboard *White Dawn*—post sinking and without the stern armor.

(photo by Peter White)

Charlie and I pulled away from the tender late in the afternoon after an 8000-pound delivery, and rumors of $.85 a pound being paid by some processors. The run seemed strong, the bugs were worked out, and we were giddy with success. We charged back to the south-line boundary with visions of glory implanted in our heads. The weather was reasonably calm and soon we laid-out the first set of a long night of steady fishing.

Sometime in the morning the wind started rising above the protection afforded by the long south beach. Peering into the fishhold brimming with salmon, I belayed any further thoughts of setting the net again. Packed with 12,000- pounds, *White Dawn's* bow was settled well down into the water—her skirts were hiked high. This was her most vulnerable posture; exposed and open to even moderate seas that wanted to climb over her forward bulwarks.

We rounded the northern end of the beach at Goose Spit, heading for our buying tender anchored on the other side of Coffee Point. Out of the lee of the beach the wind became instantly more apparent, suddenly assaulting us with a force-8 (34-40 knots) gale. The accompanying waves regularly broke over the bow, slopping disturbing amounts of water into the exposed cockpit. I slowed to the most unobtrusive speed I could find but, even with Charlie assisting at intervals with a bucket, still the pumps ran steadily.

With her valuable cargo of fish (worth more than I paid for the boat), I felt as protective, and nearly as helpless under the onslaught, as someone trying to shepherd his bitch-in-heat through a pack of wild dogs. I mightily tried to resist my darkest thoughts of a rogue wave breaking over us and plunging the boat at an uninterrupted dive to the bottom. Was this what happened to all the men, particularly in sailboats, who had died in sudden storms around this area? On the lighter points, at the moment we appeared to be on the good side of the disastrous edge, all systems were operating, and the reward for our hard work lay only a mile ahead.

We swept wide of the notorious Coffee Point tide-rip I'd come to know so well with the *Rebel*, but found little relief on the other side. Though the fetch of the sea was reduced from the narrowing river, the waves were still steep and uncomfortably high. I called the captain of our tender. He assured me he could offer us one protected side to offload on by jogging his 90-foot boat at an angle into the seas sweeping across the wide river. I measured his words as I heard the sound of the wind above the engine noise, and saw it grab the tops of the dynamic waves that erupted on our starboard beam. The bursts soared high for a brief moment, to be snatched by the gale and sent whisking sideways downwind. The shattered water mixed with the curtain of spray left hanging from the breakers exploding on the shore close off our port side. We were braced hard against the excessive roll as we stared through the distorted view offered by the ineffective wipers. Appearing slowly out of the gale, at last loomed the hulking black steel of our tender—the *Massacre Bay.*

Pulling near the house-aft crabber, I was puzzled by a large, beamy wooden skiff straining on its painter tied to the stern rail. How it got there in this weather, or to whom it belonged, was a mystery that was partially solved when we eased alongside and I saw a hip-booted gal, possibly a marooned setnetter, step out on deck.

I craned my neck at the bridge windows fifteen-feet above us and received a thumbs-up from the captain. He appeared intent on jogging the big scow into the waves at a 45-degree angle as promised. These same waves erupted on the beach 200 yards behind us. Not willing to commit us foolishly, I rode close alongside the *Massacre Bay,* contemplating whether our cleats would survive the up-and-down surge with the additional weight of the fish pulling on them. With the protection the lee side provided, it looked possible.

We threw extra long lines over, extending them as far fore-and-aft along the dark hull as we could. When we were secured, their deck crane hovered over us like a hungry raptor while we got ready to clip the first 1000-pound brailer bag of fish onto the swinging hook.

The popping crane cable and groaning tie-up lines added more audible turmoil to the surging stage we tried to balance on; potential disaster lurked in each moment.

We had two brailers lurched successfully over the rail when I glanced over and saw the captain himself fussing with something on deck. I wondered who the hell was at the helm! Jerking my head up to look at the bridge windows, I connected

44

with the stricken face of the setnet woman wrestling frantically with the big wheel. As if in the middle of a nightmare, where powerlessness is the core of the horror, I watched the bow of the *Massacre Bay* swing steadily through the wind.

Instantly, we were in a far different world. The *White dawn* was caught on the top of a curling wave and slammed unmercifully against the steel hull. Charlie and I hit the deck hard, thrown violently against the combing. The next wave wrenched us away with the accompanying snap of a whip as the three-quarter inch bowline broke. The next wave picked us up high and swung the bow out away from the hull. We watched helplessly. On the peak of the wave, like a wrestler positioning us perfectly in preparation for a body slam, we were spun stern toward the dark wall. I grabbed my knife and was futilely clawing aft to cut the stern line when we rocketed backward, slamming into the unforgiving *Massacre Bay* with unbelievable force. The ramming bar took the full brunt of the blow—making the strangely appropriate cracking sound of breaking bone at the huge impact. The engine died. I jumped below and gaped at the bizarre sight of seawater pouring into the boat; a shocking sight that just wasn't supposed to happen! Ducking low I could see a broad cascade of water gushing through the lowest transom plank. I tried to restart the engine, but the starter was already submerged.

For a moment I held to some illusion of salvation by staying tied to the *Massacre Bay,* but there was no way in this weather. No, shallow water was our only hope. Grabbing the packet of ship's papers, I threw them over the railing of our unwitting assassin and cut the stern line. Our course of action sealed, Charlie and I put on our lifejackets and jumped below into the rising water, stuffing what we could into garbage bags and rode the wind and seas toward the chaos on shore.

We were so heavy in the water when we went through the first set of breakers, there wasn't the violence I would have expected—just the brief impact of the wave and a firm, accelerated surge that sluggishly surfed us toward the beach. Surrounded by whitewater, we climbed to the outhouse roof and clung to the antenna mounts. At the inner set of waves the sea engulfed the top of the cabin just as the boat grounded. I knew the water was cold, but had so much adrenaline pumping through me I didn't notice.

I told Charlie it was time to go. He stepped into the surf in all his bulky gear and half-swam, half-flailed his way safely to shore. I secured the floating end of our net to the cabin and, in a final act of surrender, abandoned my boat—watching *White Dawn's* antennas disappear as I dropped into a trough and kicked my way toward the beach.

•

We were not left in our bedraggled state for long. Shar zoomed-up presently in a truck, responding to a radio call frantically repeating, "The boys are on the beach, the boys are on the beach!" I wanted to stay near the boat, but was finally persuaded to dry off and regroup at her cabin.

From the optimistic view, the timing of the sinking was perfect. The high tide placed us well onto the sand flats and started to ebb just as we stepped off the boat. Sure enough, when we drove up later, *White Dawn* sat claiming the flats for herself.

We were rested, warm and well stocked with rescue equipment. Walking to the stern I could see the damage clearly. In absorbing the impact of the collision, the diagonal support struts of the ramming halo had transferred the energy down to the plank it was bolted to, splitting the fine cedar grain of the wood as sure as a watermelon husk. I could fit half my hand into the crack stretching seven-feet across the stern.

With a blast of revitalized energy we pumped the boat dry, delivered the 3000 pounds of fish remaining in the boat to a pick-up truck, and bent to the task of repairing the transom. First was the satisfying job of ripping off the heavy steel ramming protection. I swear I heard her sigh when relieved of the heavy armor. The split plank closed nicely when we jacked the stern up from below and scabbed a silicon-smeared patch of plywood over the wound—not pretty, but effective.

I called my friend Jon Crooks on a borrowed CB radio and asked him if he would be willing to perform a rescue off the beach at high tide, the darkest hour of the night. We had met that winter king crabbing out of Dutch Harbor, each looking for adventure and trying to bolster our financial bases. It seemed appropriate that two young guys with old wooden boats (his was a double-ended Bristol Bay sailboat converted to power about the time of *White Dawn's* arrival) should make this happen.

At 01:30 *White Dawn* floated off the sand and started to restlessly jerk on her anchor. The first waves from a barely diminished wind rolled in with the tide. It still blew 30-knots. It quickly became more uncomfortable, especially without the insurance of power, as the wind's effect reached farther in. I was extremely concerned how Jon was going to get in without endangering himself. Attentive to our situation, many of the tenders in the channel turned their crab lights our way and lit up the night for us. Then—through the eerie backdrop of blackness mixed with artificial light, which highlighted the spindrift blowing off the wave tops—Jon appeared heroically atop a wave surfing straight toward us. Appearing as if he did this every day, he pirouetted around on the spent wave, tossed a buoy with a line attached our way and jogged into the still dangerous remains of the next breaker. In a moment we had the buoy alongside and the line tied-off. I signaled Jon to take up the strain. With the guttural noise of his own laboring Chrysler Crown bellowing above the din, he timed our escape flawlessly, hauling us away from the beach and out through the threatening surf to safety.

•

There was mechanical work and an ugly amount of clean-up required while we tied-up to the cannery at the village of Egegik where Jon deposited us. In an exchange of courtesy with our own cannery in Naknek, the New England cannery offered needed parts and useful advice. Charlie took care of the mechanics; I tried to get the oil, grease and bilge water marinade out of the mattresses and other equipment. Pilot biscuits and peanut butter sufficed as our bland nourishment for most meals.

Each evening I half-heartedly checked in with Jon to see what fishing we had missed that day. Luckily, we were on the downside of the heavy peak fishing and the reports could have been much more painful. I experienced a certain calm resignation that I had acquired from a season with *Rebel* watching too many fish swim by while sitting on the beach. With the carburetor re-installed and a semblance of normality regained, we were running and ready to go on the third day.

We made the very best of the remainder of the season, and ended in strong seaworthy form. Shar and I put the boat back on the dock after an exciting pink salmon fishery in August. Charlie would drift-fish with me again, but soon embarked on another successful fishing career—anchored securely on the beach as a setnetter.

•

There is a type of primal soul connection one establishes with a wooden boat, and *White Dawn* was no exception. She was built with loving hands, took care of us well, didn't ask for much, and earned our trust and respect. I would have been sorry to miss the experiences with her.

I fished her another season, and she was the platform from which we launched our next step forward. This would be into the specialized world of the budding aluminum fishing boat revolution—boats more suited for the rock and roll fishery that some areas of Bristol Bay were evolving into. *White Dawn* was better suited for other areas where she could be the lady most suited to her design.

Last I saw her, she waltzed out of the dance bound for another party, lingering for a moment to flip up her skirt, revealing the fine curves of her bottom I would often miss.

CHAPTER 4

WIND, WAVES, AND CHATS WITH GOD

≈

Sail forth—steer for the deep waters only,
Reckless O soul. exploring, I with thee, and thou
with me,
For we are bound where mariner has not yet dared
to go,
And we will risk the ship, ourselves and all.
O my brave soul!
O farther, farther sail!
O daring joy, but safe! are they not all the seas of
God?
O farther, farther, farther sail!

—Walt Whitman

The world around me was in savage cold chaos. Howling gale winds whipped the tops off steep breaking seas, lashing *Vulcan*—our spanking new aluminum fishing boat—as she lay broadside, rolling violently from the waves sweeping underneath. The engine had died, the fuel tank empty, and I was alone. I was being blown incredibly fast towards the steep cliffs on the shore. Even through the din of the wind, I could hear the boom of each wave hitting the wall like cannon fire from a Man-of-War. I was close enough to see the spray shoot fifty feet into the air over the snow-shrouded rocks. When the engine quit, I had immediately dropped the anchor and let out all the line wrapped on the winch spool—but it still hung straight down, mocking my earnest intentions. The chart showed 100 feet of water close to the base of the rocks on this exposed section of the Canadian Inland Passage. I knew the anchor would never grab in time to prevent *Vulcan's* stout 32-foot hull from being pounded into an unrecognizable 20,000 pound chunk of crunched aluminum...I had maybe ten minutes to get out of this one.

•

I chose to take the boat alone from Seattle for the first 750 miles of this one-month, 2700-mile maiden voyage to our fishing grounds in Bristol Bay, Alaska, for the 1980 season. The hurried work prior to leaving on the journey north involved so much outward 'doing' that I wanted to reconnect with the neglected inner 'being' part of myself. What better salve for the soul than quiet anchorages and the extraordinary scenery of the beautiful Inland Passage?

Starting in the benign mid-March Northwest weather, the plan for the expedition was to drive north and west to the Bering Sea, where much of North America's harshest weather is born. The Bay tucks snugly into the southeast corner of the Bering Sea, and plays host to the greatest wild sockeye salmon run in the world.

This 'pleasure' cruise would take us through some of the most spectacular country on the planet, and I was hoping to share most of it with my partner and wife, Shar, who would be patiently waiting for me on the dock in Ketchikan two days from now. She would be pissed if I couldn't show up.

•

Although I was solo, there was no dearth of company inside my head.

Well, you've done it now you bloody FOOL! This will teach you to be so cheap.

I had aborted my last fuel stop at a sleepy Canadian village on Sunday morning. I thought the guy manning the fuel dock was smirking when he refused to give me the 30% currency exchange rate. I checked the sight gauge at the tank and calculated I would have four hours extra fuel after reaching Prince Rupert, Canada. I had a barrel of fuel in the stern, but a poor plan for getting it out in an emergency. I badly wanted to blame the tank capacity that was perhaps incorrectly reported, or the new engine that was suddenly slurping too much fuel, but the voice was now screaming hysterically how totally responsible and wrong I was. Next, fear elbowed in.

Yup, you push and push things to the edge and now you're probably going to get hurt and lose this boat you and Shar worked four long years to buy!

As one tends to do when times are desperate and one feels like a crumbled, frightened heap of humility, I chatted with God. I was quick, but fervent.

I know we don't talk enough, and I've surely had more than my fair share of chances, but Great Spirit I could use a hand pulling my sorry butt out of here.

Fortunately, the commanding voice in charge of survival at the center of my mental cyclone recognized the need for calm and clarity. Spurred by the increasing sound of exploding surf, I grabbed tools, plus a length of garden hose, and tore off the cap to the 55-gallon fuel barrel.

YOU IDIOT! Why didn't you put an emergency hand pump at the top of the list before departing?

I stuck the small hose into the barrel and sucked with everything I had. When my mouth filled with diesel, I jammed the hose into a five-gallon bucket and the siphon started.

Retching as I lurched to the cabin, I punched channel-16 on the VHF radio and made an emergency call announcing my location and predicament. Another boat responded but he was a long half-hour away. Snatching the big funnel from a box, I staggered back across the deck and sat down in the cockpit, cradling the bucket in my lap to prevent the precious rising liquid from slopping out with the extreme roll of the boat. My mind frantically calculated the speed of drift against the agonizingly slow speed of fuel flow. I had to sit and wait. It seemed strange and Zen-like to be approaching so much potential violence with so much apparent passivity.

Finally, I was out of time. Bracing myself against the gunwale, I started to pour the accumulated fuel into the wide-mouth funnel. With deepening dread I watched the freezing wind snatch the stream and whip it away sideways. More desperate measures were necessary. Tearing my coat and shirt off, I clambered outside the railing and crouched facing the gale, locking the funnel between my knees with my stomach jammed against the rim. The deep roll was increasing and becoming more violent from the waves bouncing off the thundering shore 200 yards away! Using my torso as a funnel extension, I poured the diesel on my chest between my hunched shoulders and watched most of it flow down my body into the tank. I resumed my conversation while crawling back to the cabin.

I have no reasonable reason to expect this diesel engine to start without lengthy priming but, unfortunately, I am COMPLETELY out of time and promise to try and be smarter if I could get this LITTLE BIT OF HELP!

I turned the key—the engine started!!! Here was the first of a number of strange, unexplained mysteries/miracles that occurred on the voyage.

The seas smashing against the sheer rock wall close by the starboard side sent shock waves that reverberated off the boat as I idled off the frenzied shore into nearby shelter. Noticing blood on the wheel, I stared at the gash on my hand, laughing out loud at this gentle reminder of my hastily promised vows.

•

That evening over a glass of rum, I had a stern personal talk with myself. I was disgusted over the stupid decision I made at the fuel dock. It seemed my discernment of healthy and unhealthy risks had not improved much since I was a boy. I remembered sitting in the middle of my room and dropping a lit match into a quart jar full of firecrackers. I wanted to see if I could blow it out in time. After the last explosions subsided, my frightened and very angry mother found me in the corner, rolled in crash position. She was not any happier later in the day when the hastily cleaned-up, unexploded crackers went off while she was burning the trash. I certainly learned a good deal in both instances, there just had to be safer ways to acquire the answers I craved.

•

The MARCO shipyard in San Diego, building fine quality vessels for fishing fleets around the world, built *Vulcan* for the herring and salmon fisheries in Bristol Bay. Competition in the Bay was increasing. She was a forerunner for many others, and marked the first big wave of higher powered, larger capacity vessels that would change the flavor of the Bay forever.

We named the boat after the mythological Greek God *Vulcan,* the great blacksmith who forged lightening bolts on his anvil for his father, Zeus. Eventually, he was thrown out of heaven for dallying with one of his father's mistresses. He landed hard—a mortal with a gimp leg—but became an honored friend to Man as a toolmaker. I appreciated him as a role model for the latter part of his mythic existence, and related to him through my own blacksmithing hobby.

•

Vulcan in Glacier Bay.

Two days after the 'incident', I pulled up to the airport float across the channel from Ketchikan just a Shar's jet landed. I filtered the out-of-fuel story into the conversation as she flitted about the boat happily inspecting and touching all the equipment and new comforts like a child in her first house. It seemed as if I was going to get off easy until she paused for a moment. She turned and looked at me with an omniscient stare and said, "I was wondering why you smelled like diesel. So," she went on, "you've been playing too close to the fire again?" And after a long moment, "Besides your life, which I'm glad you saved, we have a lot more at stake now. You could have burned us both this time."

After the *Rebel* and the *White Dawn*, we were ecstatic at the comfort of the new ride. While the galley table was bolted to the top of the exposed engine on the *White Dawn*—admittedly an effective method of keeping the soup warm—*Vulcan* sported a table that could set four, a refrigerator, and an always hot oven that would soon be emitting delicious smells from Shar's latest baked creations. Additionally, the boat had dry comfortable bunks and a hot shower. And, oh yes!, the days of dealing with bodily functions squatting on a bucket in the rain were history.

●

The late March weather was generally cold and beautiful running up the channels of the Inside Passage. Canada and the U. S share approximately one thousand miles of this unique water highway. It appears that some great tectonic event caused the coast to shatter away from the mainland, freezing in mid-collapse, leaving a ribbon of channels, fiords, and hidden bays at the fracture lines. A close cousin to Chile's Patagonia, it is a magical coastline with a long early American cultural history. Everywhere, quiet anchorages shared by mountain goats, eagles, bears, and killer whales provided rich character to the backdrop of powder white, majestic mountains juxtaposed against the dense green forests below.

Gray whales, migrating north from their nursery lagoons in Baja, swam with their young in the deep open waters outside of us. Also plying the deep waters were the early barges bringing the eagerly awaited freight north. They paralleled the few early northbound fishing boats we saw on the inside route; everyone on their way to the start of some fishing season along the lengthy water byways of Alaska.

•

In the fall following the season ahead of us, Shar and I had an intimate encounter with one of the 270' X 70' barges. Great engineless platforms hauled by powerful tugs, they are capable of transporting tremendous loads of stacked vans, boats and equipment.

We had just finished delivering coho salmon to our 90-foot tender. We were secured to his starboard (right) side. I was talking with the captain on his aft deck when a dark shadow cast over us as if a storm cloud had suddenly stopped in front of the sun. Looking up, we saw the 25-foot high black wall of an out-of-control barge careening across the five-knot tide towards the tender's port side of the tender. I leapt over the rail onto *Vulcan's* deck, frantically yelling for Shar, waiting on the bow, to untie the line. Grabbing my knife, I cut the stern line through at the moment of the collision. As one would whack an opponents croquet ball off into oblivion, the terrific impact on the opposite side launched our ten-ton boat five feet sideways in the water. I was thrown over the rail, managing to grab hold on the way by, ending up dangling in the water. Shar somehow held on to the bow handrails against the snapping whiplash.

The barge, attached to a tug desperately powering against the tide, had broken loose in the swift water and snapped around in a crack-the-whip fashion against the steel tender. The damage, though not crippling, was a badly caved-in forward beam section, and frayed nerves all around. Had we been on the side of the crash, it would have accordioned our hull, cracked the aluminum welds, and probably sent us to the bottom!

•

Viewed on the chart, our course through the islands took on a peculiar zigzagged look. Our guiding philosophy on this leg was, 'Strike while the iron is hot', or translated, 'soak in every hot spring we can find'. In this quest, the shortest route was frequently sacrificed.

At the northern end of the Passage sits Glacier Bay National Park and Preserve. It tucks against the comforting breast of the magnificent Fairweather Mountains like a well-protected maternal charge. The Park can easily be described as a spiritually enchanting experience, particularly in the quiet of early spring. We idled in slowly so as not to disturb the pervading silence filling the numerous ice-filled bays.

Poking around numerous bays, we took the opportunity to jump in the freezing water and test out our survival suits—full body, rubber dry- suits that give one a 'Gumby' appearance. This was the welcomed new fashion statement in survival wear that would save the lives of many seamen in the coming years. If they are donned in time, the suits offer the only real hope of extended survival in the frigid northern waters. Suited up and splashing crazily around the boat, the circling sea lions could not figure out what demented sea creatures we represented.

The ancient ice on the face of the glaciers was the most extraordinary blue—like the secret unblinking eye of the universe. One morning we blew up our two-person toy raft and paddled near shore, some distance from the 60-foot vertical face of a glacier. With a tremendous, deep-throated groan, 100 feet of the face calved-off and toppled slow motion into the water. For an instant we were spellbound at the spectacle—until I realized the wave this would produce. We frantically started to paddle toward the seeming safety of shore when I woke to the reality and yelled, "We've got to go deep!" We reversed and thrashed back the other way, looking like some retarded water bug. Panting from our exertion, the large wave rolled under us, lifting us unscathed like a fast elevator to its peak, and exploded on the shore in a fury of sound and spray.

•

We left Glacier Bay early in April, breaking though a quarter-inch of pre-dawn ice at our anchorage. Rounding Cape Spencer we picked up a 30-knot wind on our stern. Before us lay a 300 mile, day and night run across the Gulf of Alaska.

Wind, Waves, and a Suicidal Boat

It was a dark, rough night—made worse when the spotlight quit, leaving us truly blind. Our electronic navigational equipment, along with the chart, kept us headed in the right direction, but what was under the water concerned me more. Logging in Southeast Alaska left innumerable renegade logs floating loose. Eventually they absorbed enough water to half-sink and hang vertically before finally settling to the bottom. These 'deadheads' lay in wait like mines, waiting for a chance to do substantial damage to the hulls' of unsuspecting mariners who hit them. Adding insult to injury, our autopilot had failed one day out of Seattle. The horribly stiff steering, which MARCO later improved, was strictly hands-on. The constant wrestling with the wheel left us with painful shoulder ticks after each two-hour watch.

Sometime during the night we passed the remote village of Yakutat. The dawn found us abeam of the Malaspina Glacier—once as large as Rhode Island, but now melting fast, it was becoming clear, due to global warming. Adjacent to the glacier loomed the great mass of the second highest mountain in the U.S, Mount St. Elias. Its flanks soared high, topping at 18,008 feet above sea level. Rarely does one see the full height of a tall mountain starting from foot number one. Consider: at the base of Everest, what you see looking up from base camp, the real starting point, is the top 11,428 feet of the mountain's mass. Mount St. Elias was an awesome sight; I had dreamed of climbing it for years. The frazzled physical edges produced by the night melted away as the rising sun bathed the majestic scene in light.

During the morning the wind increased to 40-knots, still behind us. The cabin was frequently punctuated by exhilarated yells as we surfed at high speed down the face of the building seas. The boat was stable and showed little tendency to broach (turn sideways) when the bow plowed full speed into the valley between one wave and the beginning of the next. Mid-morning we rounded Cape St. Elias and barreled on toward Prince William Sound.

•

The stern flogging I had given myself earlier about acceptable challenges evidently did not take. I found myself ignoring the underlined warning in the Coastal Pilot, *Passage should only be attempted with local knowledge,* regarding the easterly, short cut approach through shallow water to Cordova. The Pilot strongly suggested that the prudent mariner would go the extra 40-miles around Hinchinbrook Island when entering Prince William Sound. For some bizarre reason I assumed I was local enough—perhaps justifying my sorry addiction to seeking the trail-less-traveled and worrying about the consequences later. Moreover, I was sure anyone who had spent as much time bumping the sand bars where I usually fished would have no problem negotiating the numerous bars in these waters. Besides, there was calm water behind the sand islands, and the respite from the turbulent sea would be welcomed.

The wind still moaned through the high antenna array after two hours of grinding on the bottom and fruitless roaming among the sand bars. I found myself unreasonably determined not to admit defeat. I decided to try a channel west of us.

Shar, showing great restraint in the face of my obviously serious problem, was hot on the chart, calling out depth and navigational coordinate numbers as we approached the slot. Through the years I was continually impressed with her calm capabilities when faced with dangerous situations like this. Looking ahead, beyond the wind blown breakers rolling before us, I could see enticing calm water. I was beginning to feel more confident. Suddenly the stern started to lift. My stomach sank when I heard the frightening sound that followed the motion. Jerking my head around, all I could see through the windows was a wall of water—the bottom half of a huge, cresting wave. I tried to center the stern on the monster, but we were already way out of control. With a terrifying, roaring rumble it picked us up and slowly broached us sideways and over 90-degrees. Shar, sitting across at the galley table, dropped across the cabin onto me at the helm. My body kept her from going through the starboard window that lay flat in the water. The wave buried us and the daylight disappeared.

In the moment all I could think about was how long we might survive if we could get to the survival suits and somehow make it to shore. In the grip of this omnipotent force, I was

59

experiencing an interesting feeling of surrender when, miraculously, *Vulcan* stopped rolling! She lay for a moment, and then slowly started to come back upright. Shar, her face pressed hard against mine as if in a check-to-cheek dance, pulled back an inch and with amazing calm said, "Lets get the hell out of here."

With the stern cockpit full of water, we pounded our way out through the breaking seas. We scarcely breathed as the green water from successive waves rolled over the bow and punched the cabin—each sickening thud threatening to smash the windshields and invade the boat. Still intact, we finally broke clear of the turbulent mess and immediately steered for the more traveled deep-water route into Prince William Sound. It was a clear understatement to say we were starting to fall in love with the boat.

After a long period of reflective silence, I noticed crackers neatly lined up in the window drip-gutter by my shoulder and thanked Shar for the thoughtful appetizer presentation. She reminded me that, last seen, the crackers had been on the port side table and that, since I continually insisted on living by Nietzsche's creed of 'that which does not kill me strengthens me', I should not expect that kind of service for a while. "And, I really wish" she continued, "if you must practice this philosophy, do it alone—or better, get some therapy!"

•

Shar has an uncanny ability to rouse herself from a deep sleep in perfect time to prevent nasty surprises (like drifting boats ramming us in the night) or to observe extraordinary things. This night it was the latter. Secure in a beautifully protected cove near Prince William Sound, big enough for perhaps two boats, she nudged me to come up and enjoy a spectacular northern lights show. It was crispy cold. Stretched across the black velvet sky, waving like a giant curtain within seeming reach just above our heads, the atmosphere actually hissed. The curtain displayed brilliant random rainbow colors weaving throughout the undulating folds. We watched, "ahhed and wowed" for some time, finally returning to our chilled bunk for a few hours of rest.

The peaceful beauty continued the next morning when we awoke. Our little cove was frozen solid. Gentle mist rose off the ice, creating an ethereal quality to it all.

Shattering ice played a soft crystal symphony on the hull as we eased into open water. Still idling, we passed a sea otter drifting on his back, his belly littered with pieces of shell. I leaned out the window and asked, "Hey, what's for breakfast?" In reply, he smiled and picked up the large shell of a king crab and waved it back and forth in the air like a boxer showing off an outsized, newly won championship medallion.

It would take years to fully appreciate the splendor of the Sound. It's many glaciers slowly flow down from the Chugach Mountains and end their journey in the once rich waters, now slowly healing from the polluted bath of Exxon oil, like a patient from a terrible disease. The outward beauty has returned, but the cancer hidden in the land, and in the hearts of the people, will take much longer to heal.

•

Snugly tied-up in the Homer boat harbor at the end of the four mile spit, we whittled away on the long list of work to be done. In the evenings we gathered with old friends and shared the familiar camaraderie from past Alaskan adventures. We also connected with Tom Maxwell and Robert Butt who were about to run their own new Bay boats, *Heidi* and *Renegade*, down the Aleutian Peninsula. They, too, were headed through False Pass to the Togiak herring grounds.

I was somewhat anxious about the weather reported for Shelikof Straits, a notorious wind funnel, but the forecasted winds never materialized. All three boats slipped down the Strait, between Kodiak Island and the mainland, as if on an inland lake. Droning west down the Aleutian chain past stunning Castle Cape, Chignik, and other special places known to the few who live and work there, Shar and I were overwhelmed by the wild beauty of the snow covered volcanoes and desolate shoreline. We talked about coming back and living there for a while—it was our kind of place.

The thermostat on Tom's engine broke, which ultimately meant we were forced to leave him waiting for repairs in the fishing port of Sand Point. *Vulcan*, along with Bob and Jerry onboard *Renegade*, passed through False Pass, the first place you can turn right through the long peninsula and enter the legendary Bering Sea.

For small boats that need shelter, the Bering Sea can be a scary place. Going northeast towards Bristol Bay, there is approximately 300 miles of exposed beach with only two possibilities for shelter—each about 100 miles apart.

True to the Sea's reputation, we could see scudding spindrift from a building storm blowing across the water beyond the protection of the pass. It was tempting to consider hiding in False Pass for a while, but time was growing short and the herring season was not going to wait for us. Foul weather is the norm in this part of the world, and waiting for good conditions can be like waiting for rain in the desert. Additionally, we had to acknowledge the strong two-to-three knot currents caused by the common 20-foot tidal changes flushing in and out as the Bering Sea breathed. The flood tide was our friend just as surely as the ebb tide was our enemy. Reluctantly, we decided to push on.

The wind increased to a full gale, hitting us just off the bow. Though Bob was only a few hundred feet away, we would frequently lose sight of the tops of his antennas between the waves and curling crests. Because of our short hull length, the boats would often be left high-centered and hanging in the air as the building seas rolled under. After a large wave, we might fall six feet or more before smacking into the trough. Shar lay in her bunk with a mountain of pillows over her body, protecting herself from slamming the overhead when the boat fell out from under us.

When dusk settled over us, Bob and I both throttled back to reduce the horrendous pounding and resultant spray that flew high over the boats and kept the decks wet. The temperature dropped and spray started to lightly freeze on the rigging. Unable to afford much accumulation, we prepared to beat it off with hammers. I shivered thinking of us rolling over to join the too many other much larger brethren resting on the Bering Sea floor below us.

I watched the temperature and felt my nerves stressing tighter with each falling degree. While I held on and fought our wheel (now too stiff for Shar to steer) *Vulcan* pounded on through the rough, wet night. I frequently thought of the reliable autopilot Bob had steering *Renegade* for him. My fatigued mind coveted his self-steering with an unnatural obsessiveness. Always present was an acute awareness of how small and vulnerable we were in this vast, raging sea. I tried 'willing' everything to stay functioning...but it was not to be.

At midnight the beating on our nose eased when the wind veered until it was ripping over the stern quarter. The gale was blowing harder than I wanted to calculate. At 03:00, following a tremendous, shuddering gust, the engine abruptly died! The raw emotional angst from the last abrupt stop off the rocks in Canada was still fresh in me. This silence was like re-opening a painful wound. I jerked open the engine hatch, immediately choking on a billowing cloud of smoke pouring out from below. Even with the security of *Renegade* standing by, I pictured the unforgiving coast three-miles away and could not imagine how we could possibly hook-up and maintain a tow in these seas.

All the while an analytical part of my brain was trying to evaluate the smell of the smoke. It wasn't from fire or steam? Grabbing a flashlight I jumped below and felt the air filter I had recently changed. It was plugged with black soot! Shar popped the back hatch off and cleared the smoke while I changed the filter, and *Vulcan* rolled deeply in the trough. Engaging the starter, the boat immediately roared to life. Stepping out— oblivious to the drenching spray lashing across the deck—I stared above me in disbelief at the mouth of the exhaust stack facing directly into the storm. It slowly dawned in my frayed mind that the blast of wind had somehow blown the smoke back down the stack and snuffed out the 275 horsepower diesel beast like a candle! There was no other explanation I could grasp.

•

The fishing boats tied up and comfy in Port Moller were a welcome sight. We made some repairs, explored, and rested. Hovering over us was the concern about missing the start of the fishing season (and our first boat payment). Despite the wind still blowing—though slightly abated and angling across the land—we shoved off before dawn for the next shelter twelve hours up the coast.

Late in the afternoon we arrived off Port Heiden—a remote village of hardy, mostly native, souls—and spent an hour searching for the way into the inner lagoon. It is a difficult, shifting approach, and sure enough the sand island shown off the entrance on the chart had disappeared since the last updates were made. *Vulcan* went aground outside the shallow channel along the beach. The only option was dropping the hook and waiting to float later in the night. Meanwhile, Bob waited nearby for low water and went dry next to the channel. At the bottom of the ebb we walked over and had dinner onboard *Renegade*. Using the new information we received from radio contact with the locals, we discussed strategy for getting into the protected lagoon.

During dinner, like Indians circling the wagons, the wind continued to slowly back around us. By the time Shar and I trudged back to the boat, it was shrieking onshore in the guise of a 45-knot blizzard. With *Vulcan* broadside, I was distressed at our position. We were not in a comfortable posture to face a rising tide with the accompanying merciless, breaking seas.

Near midnight the first water started to lightly spank against the hull—a fearful prelude to the potential beating that was preparing for us out in the deep darkness. I geared up against the sub-zero chill factor and positioned myself on the bow. I would use the anchor and winch to drag *Vulcan's* bow around to face the storm. The snow cut-off much of our overhead spotlight beam as it tried to pierce the darkness.

Bent against the numbing wind and stinging snow, I inched the bow around with each fresh movement of the boat. The anchor line was piano-wire taut. Just before she floated, the deepening water started to slam us with jolting force. Again and again *Vulcan* reared and slammed the bottom like a panicked wild stallion. My hand grasped the stiff line stretched between the winch and anchor-roller. Squinting, I caught a glimpse of a large wave looming out of the night. Determined to get the most as it lifted us, I slammed the hydraulic winch handle down hard. Instantly I felt excruciating pain in my hand and looked over to see half my glove buried under the tight line on the

64

spool. Reversing the winch to free my trapped hand, I felt the doubled layers start to saturate with warm blood.

Though an EMT, and generally not squeamish about spilling my own plasma, my body broke out in a hot flush of sweat; my vision started to blur. Resting my head on my arm for a moment, I fought the urge to faint. The waves were pounding us hard, and I was afraid of getting pitched off. Without any pretense of delicacy, I had Shar power full ahead until I could winch the anchor aboard. While she moved *Vulcan* into the more protected channel on the other side of the bar, I hunched over with my arm wrapped around the chain in a death-like embrace until it was time to re-anchor.

Collapsed on the galley floor, I tried to calm my desire to hyperventilate. So much depended on the use of my hands. I feared the prospect of facing the season before us with a mangled hand. We eased off the glove. The plentiful blood and torn tissue made be think the worst. But there was no bone showing, and some movement. After a thorough cleaning and inspection, we determined the damage was confined to my thumb—the bones seemed intact. The pinch of the line had popped the skin off like a grape. Gruesome as it appeared, after replacing the flesh back over the raw digit, I was confident it would heal quickly.

•

Equipped with the necessary local knowledge, we entered the Lagoon as soon as we could for a needed breather. The people in the village were forthcoming with fuel, information and friendliness, but our visit had to be brief. With assurances of a deep channel—used by the supply tugboats—straight out from the Lagoon, we took a deep breath and started the final run north. I was anxious about my steering abilities and response time working with one hand, but I wanted to be at the helm for what lay ahead.

Exiting the comfort of the Lagoon, *Vulcan* followed *Renegade* around the protected point out into the still tempestuous Bering Sea. The sight caused us severe second thoughts. The waves were huge, some twenty-feet high, tripping and viciously breaking in the shallow water. They spread both ways down the

65

exposed shore, pounding the beach as far as we could see. Focusing closer, we made out the gut and saw that the deep water in the narrow channel created a central, tight tongue of waves, minus the terrible curls and breaking crests. Going though them did not appear to be completely suicidal—only partially so.

Maybe we were tired of being beaten up, or losing the boat to the bank instead of the sea; maybe we were especially optimistic about having some divine protection—we decided to chance it.

At one point Shar and I saw *Renegade's* full 32-foot length, at a 45-degree angle to the sky, powering up the face of a giant wave. There was water still left in front of his bow and behind his stern. White knuckled and hypersensitive to any needed corrections, we went slowly up the first mountainous face. Through the windshield we watched a long, extended view of the sky, then see-sawed violently over the crest and slid down, down into the deep trough of the great wave—wondering how we were going to make it up the next one. The crashing waves, close on both sides, thundered in booming stereo. They seemed particularly angry and eager to devour us for our audacity in attempting the gauntlet. There was no more than a foot of room for error or hesitation. Finally, each up and down roller coaster ride became shorter and the extreme danger faded behind us.

That success was the beginning of the end of the relentless struggle in the Bering Sea. Since entering, it seemed we had paid stiff dues for every mile we put behind us.

The weather moderated steadily throughout the day; the wind and tide seemed to favor us with an extra push. With nearly 2700 miles of shakedown cruise behind us, we neared our homeport of Naknek. We would have time to lick our wounds and make the first herring opening, christening a successful salmon season to follow.

•

That last afternoon, as we entered Bristol Bay and cruised by the Ugashik and Egegik river mouths'—wrapped in a peaceful cocoon that unfolded as the danger disappeared astern—I felt wiser, more confident, more connected than a month before. The pain of the lessons was diminished by time, and I felt I had climbed over personal obstacles that would not need repeating again. Gazing out the windows, I marveled once again at the peace and balance that remained, like a gently receding wave, after the violent storm passed. Life reflected that same yin/yang equilibrium, and I was grateful for the opportunity to play the game.

CHAPTER 5

In the last half of the 90's, Bristol Bay started to stagger and fall from the previous, relatively profitable, 20 years. The once prolific runs of sockeye started declining. Most agree this was temporary and at least partially due to natural inter-decadal oscillations in the deep oceans coupled with, many believe, renewed interception by Russia 200 miles off their coast. At the same time the price started an uncontrolled downward slide in reaction to farmed salmon flooding traditional world markets. This is the story of a season when our worst fears started coming true.

CONFESSIONS OF A TRANSFER JUNKIE

≈

That which does not kill me, strengthens me.

—Friedrich Nietzsche

Fishing the Bay during the 1998 season was like being aboard a blimp plunging towards a fiery crash. Fishermen were desperately scrambling around the doomed craft trying to find a safe place—in this case one of six possible rivers systems to fish. Movement was slow motion because it requires 48 hours of non-fishing time to transfer from one district to another. Finally it became clear everyone was going to get hurt—safety was a cruel illusion.

How weird was it? The catch was over two million less than last year's disaster, but look at this: the Kvichak, initially declared DOA with nary a chance of opening even once,

69

suddenly goes wide open to extended fishing on July 13th! Ugashik, with a smolt out migration for this year's returning stocks so dismal Fish and Game wondered if reaching the escapement goal was even remotely possible, opened three times before the goal was miraculously reached late in July. On July 5 the Wood River in the Nushagak system, lagging in escapement by days, was suddenly slammed with 500,000 fish. The river immediately passed its escapement goal and turned the Nushagak district—the previously somewhat arthritic Grand ol' Dame, yet home to past healthy runs of all five species of salmon suckling on her life giving arteries—into the best transfer bet of the season. This despite over escaping 750,000 fish that could have been harvested.   In retrospect, the Nushagak becomes the tail section of the blimp that breaks off on impact and only partially maims those that have sought refuge there.

After 22 years the personal weirdness factor aboard Vulcan hit an all-time high. How strange to go through the season using one suit of nets; or never using more than 25% of our fishhold capacity; or reading four books in a season; or having our biggest day July 16! Additionally, and I admit I scrambled more than most on that 747, the listing on the back of our personalized 1998 T-shirt reads like the toured cities of a hot rock-n-roll band. We toured all six districts (Togiak, during herring) at least once.

•

June 10—Naknek is unusually quiet this time of year. The majority of boats still have buckets over their stacks. A number of friends have sold out—intelligent people with mature sensibilities and the kind of folks you want to fish around. They are assets to the fishery. Who will replace them? I fear others who will arrive with heavy debts, willing to sacrifice codes of behavior and perpetuate the worst elements of our fishery. Will they become part of our deepening problems instead of contributing to solutions?

June 19, transfer #1—We're in Ugashik and the first week of fishing is over. Except for a few fish caught when it blew 40-knots, it was a poor showing. Does this portend to the season ahead? We'll head up to Egegik and try for early fish, gather with the group, break out the barbecue. Our first entry into the dreaded 48-hour transfer Zone is painless.

June 25—fished two dismal openings. The fish are trickling in, mostly over the west edge of the district, killed immediately by the 700-plus boats crowding the boundary line. The south and notorious north lines are dead. This is not boding well!

June 28, transfer #2—Another head shaking Egegik opening. This river is missing many fish, and reports from the north in the Naknek/Kvichak systems are worse. Crowding into the light west-line show of fish, I am struck by the absurdity of what we are doing. We are fighting each other in high energy, competitive warfare, damaging the fish and causing wanton waste from drop-outs when we tow the nets, and round-hauling web with fish into a pile in the stern—all the while bringing out the worst in ourselves. We are directly responsible for the initial degradation of our fish. Who seems to be our last concern? Our customers! We've lost touch with our actual position in the world marketplace. Our situation resembles a game we've been playing on the boats during an ebbing tide. Without shore references we don't notice we're sipping out the river at four knots, away from the playing field—that is, until we pass an anchored boat and realize we've almost played ourselves right out of the 'real' game happening back in the river. Without more cooperation amongst ourselves and the processors, uniting as business partners in the world marketplace, we do not offer ourselves a good chance of future success.

•

In partial defense, it is the antiquated rules we fish by that have created the ugly beastliness that certain areas of our fishery have come to display. Crowd any species into a small space with limited food available and, of course, there will be some ugly behavior in response to simple hunger, or here, the heavy debt load that can come with this business. Yet our lawmakers would spank us and stand aghast that such a thing could happen. They should be flogged as well for their arrogance.

With good reason, the north-line ebb fishery of Egegik became the notorious poster child of savage greed and brutality in the 80's. When you jam 150 or more boats onto a line of good fishing less than one half mile long, each boat trying to set

71

900-feet of net for a potential haul worth over $1000, you will naturally see the ugly side of greed, anger and frustration. You will also see accidental collisions and purposeful rammings.

I remember once racing another boat on the line, each coming from opposite directions and laying net out like maniacs. We approached each other very fast and turned outside the boundaries trying to get around each other. We collided beam-to-beam, badly denting my combing and buckling a section of my deck. I stopped and stared at the damage, our position in illegal territory worth a potential $6000 fine, and finally 'got' the ridiculous situation we were in. I felt it as an observer of our fishery, and I felt it in my gut. We had been the top Trident boat two years running by being good on the north line, but I did not like who I had become. There were so many better, smarter ways to run a business, better ways to treat the fish, and ourselves.

•

After the last opening our group rafted-up to discus the copious amount of gathered information. Chief concern is the missing 2.2 ocean fish (salmon that spend two years in the ocean after leaving fresh water) that make up a substantial portion of the eastside returns. The Nushagak is less dependent on the 2.2 fish, and it seems the Wood River is picking up bit. With varying degrees of mind tweaking and gut wrenching pain, we transfer over to the Nushagak. I can feel this insidious financial fear creeping in. How will the debts be paid? The warrior in me is willing to stay and fight, but he would rather be saving damsels in distress and knows this Egegik battle is not the right one to be fighting.

We use the downtime in different ways. Some captains can't sit still and continually scout the district for fish and some assurance that there will be reward for the sacrifice of fishing time. The majority head up the Wood River to Aleknagik Lake for mountain climbing and a blissful world among the singing loons. We feel a million miles away from the Bay. After our time here, I know the shock of returning downstream will be no less than the cold water hitting my body after the hot sauna. Heading back down I look astern at the 'For Sale' sign on our island property. It tangibly represents my first step into the economic survival zone.

Reports from our tireless scouts in the outer river are not good: light shows of jumping fish only on the ebb, the wood and Nushagak rivers slipping further behind their needed escapements, and the test boat reports are not increasing. Nobody is fishing except Egegik. They have an 1800# per boat average from the last period, and falling. All action in the Bay is stopped. Four of us decide to fly the Bay with Karl Spielman to get an overview of how the Big game is unfolding.

Though warned of the dangers of a 'snapshot' look at the Bay, I am convinced the jumpers we see heading for the Naknek/Kvichak will become the big hit we need. My transfer demon, an especially evil and handicapped part of my ego, is rubbing its hands together in glee. Am I more affected by the strong responsibility I feel to make money for the crew and pay my own bills, or too swayed by my twisted transfer demon who sometimes manages to short-circuit common sense with promises of glory? Then, too, I am cursed with the fear of an unchallenging path in life. I feel I've lost touch with my fishing instincts. A distant quiet inner voice whispers be patient. The transfer junkie shouts FEED MY NEED.

<u>July 3, transfer #3</u>—We enter the Zone again. We're the only one going to Naknek, trying to go towards something fresh instead of backtracking; three others are returning to Egegik. Taran, my 15-year-old son, onboard for his first full season, looks at me as if I'm an idiot. This does not help my lightness-of-being. I think if emotions were the clubs in a golf bag—with the sand-wedge representing hopeless gloom and the driver adrenaline pounding ecstasy—I'll be playing with the fat sand wedge today.

Pulling away from the Bay Rose, I look at the forlorn expression on the face of my longtime fishing partner, Keith. "So, Lone Wolf," he asks, "are we ever going to fish together again?" I have no good answer.

Rule #1 in fishing Bristol Bay: never be in the transfer zone on July 4. We zigzag across the Bay on the way over looking for fish, find some jumpers. Will it be enough?

Coming into Naknek River last year at this time, we found frustrated, angry fishermen—this year it is quiet as a tomb. I sense a numbness pervading the huddled groups gathered on the back decks—a reasonable reaction to the dark storm bearing down on us all for the second year in a row.

July 4, transfer #4—I spoke with the local biologists. They indicated that it would take a small miracle for the Kvichak to catch-up on needed escapement. Naknek will probably fish the in-river special harvest area for the season, and opening will not occur very often. I am filled with sickening dread at the report. We HAVE to get the net in the water and Egegik, the only river fishing, seems like the best of a very bad situation. With the district in a rest period, we won't lose anymore fishing time, but that doesn't alleviate the agony of the decision. I look to Mike, my ever patient, long time first mate extraordinaire, but he trusts we will come out standing and, other then acting as a sounding board, will not interfere with my decision making. As I transfer, I feel as if I have a terrible drug habit and have to go back to the only dealer in town, who I know is selling bad dope. I'm back with the sand-wedge in hand.

The support from our processors has been good. We're all suffering in this together. Price talk is reflecting some optimism with the low projected volume. Still, I'm reminded that we permit holders own the rights to the salmon. Along with greater fishermen and processor cooperation and speaking with a unified voice, we need business agreements—based on revenue sharing—that fit our new relationship better than the current secretive, archaic system.

July 5—What! The report this morning informs us that 500,000 fish suddenly bolted up the Wood River. The transfer demon is screaming for an immediate transfer, or is that the voice of good instinct? Follow-up reports reveal fairly light fishing. Maybe the wad has been shot in a tide or two? I cannot handle being in the Zone again at this date; I will not feed the junkie. The music has stopped; the games about to begin, grab a river, stick and stay, make it pay. We will make our stand in Egegik.

July 6—Naknek opens in-river on the fish we saw heading in two days before. Reports are poor. Threats are made to move Egegik's west boundary into the 110-loran line as the Kvichak slips to one-third of last year's escapement at this time.

Reaching its goal is extremely unlikely. The Nushagak is still on its feet, decent fish now being caught—wish we were there.

The wind is blowing 30 knots into the Egegik River. A bottle is past quietly round the cabin. We hope the wind will blow the missing fish in. One especially superstitious partner blows up his plastic honey bear dispenser. He thinks the sacrifice of the land animal will appease the obviously angry fish gods. Egegik opens in the dark for four hours. I'm lucky and tee-off with a 3-wood. We experience intense momentary pleasure watching good hits on the net. However, the game here is soon clear: make the first set count or it will be a slow, boring period.

While waiting to deliver we watch a gillnetter with no reel hanging behind a dry scow tender. They're picking the last stressed fish from the round-hauled net. I look at our bright, refrigerated fish. Hopefully all those #2's and #3's are going into the can. These fish are just beautiful looking when they come out of the water—we can do better keeping them that way.

July 8, transfer #5—Egegik is still horribly light, and the district will shrink next opening when the west-line is pulled in. The Kvichak appears to be officially doomed.

The true cost of my two wrong decisions (leaving the Westside, and then not going back immediately) comes avalanching down on me. It seems being late for the right game would have been smarter. I blocked my instincts and broke nearly every immutable personal rule for the greedy proselytizing of the transfer junkie. In seasons past the mistakes would have been a small blip; this year the cost will be over one-third of our catch. Fearful thoughts of how to pay the mortgage and child support shift to whether we'll even make basic expenses. I philosophize that the end of something is always the beginning of something else. With dark resignation we enter the Zone yet again—back to the Nushagak. Hand me that sand-wedge again, please.

July 11—Our second day of steady fishing around-the-clock. Tuning into the river brings simplicity of purpose that is good tonic for the angst, and healing for the soul. Letting go of the attachment to the fear of loss, and the unknown future, brings a feeling almost serene.

Wind, Waves, and a Suicidal Boat

The patient Ugashik diehards got one decent opening yesterday. Can the river afford the hit? Egegik is picking up a little. But what's this on the radio about the Kvichak escapement climbing fast?

July 12—Unbelievable! The Kvichak has evidently found its miracle push of fish. The loyal Naknek fishermen rush out of the cramped river for the rare opportunity of open district fishing. I hope they score big, because the news is so good the entire Naknek/Kvichak district will be open to free transfers into the area tomorrow.

July 13—We left the Nushagak four hours before a closure and drove to the Kvichak with visions of hitting our own 10000# home run, as some lucky ones did yesterday. But, of course, the fish have been mopped up and our expedition turned into merely observation—and burning more fuel.

July 16—Back in the Nushagak. We pulled the driver out of the bag for the first time this season. In the early dawn hours, we stumbled onto a brief, thick pulse of fish and a taste of the joys of fishing. It felt good calling the group over and finally contributing something of value.

July 18—Now we've fished them all! We're wandering around the Kvichak trying to scrape up what we can of the last of this painful calamity.

Nushagak will close down soon to protect the silver salmon that appear to be copying the overall weakness of the sockeye run.

Ugashik, after three openings, will sit until the end of July, and will end with an unexpected bang with they do open.

Egegik will fade out slowly like an old movie, leaving frustrated customers with a shortage of popcorn.

We will fish for another ten days and, amazingly, come out above average. Meanwhile, the Bay catch numbers will be worse then last year. Bristol Bay has seen worse a few times in the past 30 years, but our competitors have never been stronger, nor our cost-per-pound of harvesting higher.

The final good news from the season is that all minimal escapement goals were met. That is the smart, valuable gift for the future we have assured for ourselves and, coupled with courageous changes now, it offers great hope for us.

•

So, what do we do now? Thinking globally, we can hope that the dearth of fish is a naturally occurring cycle in the deep ocean, and not the result of an oceanic sickness brought about by the hand of man. Closer to home, we can keep pressuring to find the truth about any interception of our far journeying fish. We need to start embracing a new game plan that is market driven instead of production driven. We need to change the regulations that will allow us to redirect the competition with each other into cooperation. We need to extend that cooperation and trust to the processors, and begin speaking with a unified voice. We need to spur the State of Alaska into supporting our important industry from ADF&G and ASMI budgets to low interest fishermen loans directed at improving quality. We need to be brave and redesign the fishery in such a way that serves the health of the fish, fishermen and customers in the best possible way. We can do whatever it takes to harvest these pristine salmon swimming in the water and serve them to the world markets in high quality condition.

•

The weird 1998 season was true to the end. Our last day while fishing in the Naknek district, reeling in our first empty net of the season, we were surprised by the surrealistic vision of a walrus swimming by the boat. Was he scouting for new mollusks to suck down? I thought we weren't very different: each trying to make the adjustments necessary to survive our dramatically changing worlds—and survive we will.

<u>CHAPTER 6</u>

THE FIRST DAY

≈

Sickness is the mother of modesty, putteth us
in mind of our mortality...She pulleth us by the ear,
maketh us know ourselves.

—Robert Burton,
The Anatomy of Melancholy

Over a dawn breakfast before our first Bristol Bay king salmon opening, I had mixed feelings looking beyond the protection afforded by our anchorage. Across the wide Nushagak river mouth extending beyond Clarks Point, I could see whitecaps, and spindrift was gusting across the water. It was blowing damn hard.

Rough conditions were certainly desired for bringing the big Chinook salmon to the surface and into our gillnets, but a rough first day made it hard to work out the cobwebs on the boat. Another important focus of the day was to teach Smitty how to work the deck. As for my new crewman, I never imagined anything could ruffle him.

•

Smitty was a big, solid man with a kindly heart and a cheerful temperament. Born and raised in Texas, he loved the similar spaciousness he found in Alaska. What struck people was his body THICKNESS, made so by the well-defined muscles of a dedicated weight lifter. I always imagined he was a direct descendent of the powerful blacksmiths of old from whence his last name, Smithy, came from. I felt it fitting that he eventually came to work on my Bristol Bay gillnetter, *Vulcan*—named after the great mythological blacksmith.

His strength became clear a few days before when we launched and moored in the Dillingham harbor. We tied up on the outside of seven other boats stacked all the way to the dock. "Smitty," I said stepping off the boat, "I want to swap the 8D main batteries for new ones. I'll be back in an hour to help. These are not your usual car batteries. They're a hellishly awkward grunt, even for two men."

"Roger, captain." he replied in his eternally polite manner.

When I returned, I noticed two old batteries sitting on the dock. The situation became clear when I clambered over the boats and saw the familiar grin on Smitty's face. He had single-handedly hauled the batteries out of the corner of the engine room, crossed the gauntlet of gear-strewn boats to the dock, and returned with new replacements. These were now secure in their boxes!

He had spent a number of summers working on the beach gang at the Whitney Fidalgo cannery in Naknek where I first met him. Always available, he worked hard, and everyone depended on him as part of the important link they relied on when moving their boats and gear across the docks to and from the water. Talking one morning, he indicated a desire to see what working on a boat was all about. A season later I had a crew opening and happily signed him up for the spot.

•

Early in June the Department of Fish and Game, satisfied with their upriver escapement numbers, finally announced the long awaited first king opening: a juicy twelve-hour period. We headed out, anchoring in the protected lee of the point the night before the excitement was to begin.

After our breakfast, stowing my misgivings, we secured the cabin, hauled the anchor, and rounded the point. Immediately spray was flying high over the top of the rigging and deck, hitting the windshield with steady wicked lashes. We received a thorough thrashing pounding through the waves, but finally reached the area where I wanted to start the period.

Smitty and I bundled up against the cold wetness and stepped out onto the back deck, hoods up and hunched against the gale. Tossing the buoy, I set the net as slowly as possible to prevent potential backlashes: ugly tangles that stopped the large hydraulic spinning reel dead on a set. The resulting damage could destroy a net.

We were sloshing around in water up to our ankles from the waves bursting through the transom scupper holes. The stern surged up and down so violently we had to guard the web, making sure it didn't jump out and impale itself on one of the two upright roller fairleads that guided it over the stern.

But holy shit, the fishing was good! We watched at least two hard, explosive hits every minute when strong fresh kings collided with the web and valiantly fought. We retired happily to the cabin to make a quick cup of tea.

Needing to take the time during the haul-back to show Smitty the techniques of picking fish, I reluctantly started hauling back the gear a little early. The noble twenty-five pound kings offered a magnified picture of what it would be like removing smaller sockeye from the web in a few weeks.

•

Smitty had a hard time actualizing the meaning of finesse. Granted, it was hard to stand up as we staggered around the cockpit with fish cradled in our arms, but his unwavering strategy, despite my exhorting, remained a brutal frontal attack on the gilled fish. The heavy king web seemed to magically dissolve under his hands, leaving jagged, gaping holes in the web where each fish had just been. However, I had seen grizzly bears fillet and skin sockeye like experienced chefs, and was optimistic Smitty, with similar strength, could acquire the delicate touch, too.

The wind was pressing the boat hard. I had to shift in and out of reverse to keep the net slack as we reeled it in on the big hydraulic drum. We had half the gear aboard when Smitty grabbed a 40-pounder that came over the roller. It was double gilled and twisted in a bag of web. I had a vision of a car-size hole if he had his way with this king's removal. I jumped in to assist. A moment later, on our knees, bent head-to-head, the appalling sound of tearing web under the boat pierced the drone of the wind. Before I could shift into neutral the engine died— choked into silence by unknown fathoms of web and line that had wrapped around the reversing propeller. I looked over the stern and saw the net disappearing under the heaving transom.

"I screwed up badly," I said turning to Smitty, "but don't worry. Better screw in the scupper covers, we need to clear most of the water off the deck." Then, moving toward the cabin to fetch my special knives, I yelled to myself "Captain idiot, God help us all if you could ever keep more than one thought in your head at a time!"

Whether because of chaotic, crowded conditions in Bristol Bay, or plain stupidity, 'eating' the net with the propeller is not an uncommon occurrence. Most well equipped Bay boats have an eight-inch inspection port installed directly over the prop.

I jerked the lazarette hatch off and worked my way down into the cramped space until I was lying over the port. The sound of the wind was replaced with the slow beat of the waves pounding the aluminum transom next to my head. Though the port was below the waterline, a flexible waterproof sleeve extended up from the opening when the lid was unscrewed.

"Smitty," I yelled above the bonging, "you'll have to hold the sleeve up to keep the water out while I work on the net."

"Okay, captain." came the distant voice before his arm reached down and grabbed the lip of the material.

Throwing my hood back, I reached my arm into the surging hole, and felt a tight tangled mass of corks, line, and web wrapped around the stainless blades. There was even a fish tail sticking out the side of the large blob. I cursed myself some more.

Vulcan was lurching up and down on the net like an unsettled beast. I estimated we had an hour-and-a-half windblown drift before reaching the crashing surf on the near shore. Fueled by this knowledge, and anger, I worked feverishly nonstop for over an hour cutting and hacking at the mess.

I had the blades nearly clear, and the boat out of danger, when the occasional drip from the open hatch above me turned into a steady stream of creamy, yellow liquid. It landed on my exposed neck and made its way down my back, into my ear and along my cheek.

"What the hell?" I gasped. Snapping my head out of the hatch I found Smitty, his mouth agape, eyes glazed, helplessly rolling back and forth across the deck in a huge puddle of his own vomit. The only thing keeping the big man from rolling all the way across the cockpit was the dutiful grip he still maintained on the inspection sleeve. On his next roll he saw me staring at him. He sounded terribly drunk when he gurgled weakly, "I'mmm sooo sorrry." The big man looked so vulnerable and pathetic as the deck tilted and he rolled away again. He was back facing me on the return. With great effort he said, "Iff I'mmm seasssiick tomorrrow, pleeease killl meee."

"Ah well," I said, "its only our first day."

CHAPTER 7

NOTE: *Between seasons Shar and I frequently gravitated back to the water. Being an Alaskan captain, and familiar with some of the nastiest waters in the world, I acted unwisely and let my guard down when sailing off the benign waters of Portugal. Another unexpected adventure was about to begin.*

A MARINER'S NIGHTMARE

≈

A sailboat is the living creation of the expeditionary, not the warrior; for the sea is not a cruel adversary, but an unforgiving wilderness— beautiful and awesomely powerful.

—Lawrence White,
The meaning of Sailing

The red and purple colors just recently reflected in the glassy ocean dissolved with the setting sun. Shadows were beginning to meld into the pervading darkness. It was 21:30hrs. in the still evening of October 27. We were off the coast of Portugal onboard *Witchery*, a graceful, thirty-five foot Hinkley yawl that belonged to my father. Earlier in the warm afternoon, acting on reports of potential rough water on the sandbars outside the entrance of Aviero, Shar and I had sailed past the Portuguese port. This decision prevented us from exercising our usual habit of anchoring in daylight when coastal cruising, but the weather was clear and stable. Following a brief discussion, we decided to continue. Still heading south, roughly half-way down the exposed west coast of the long country, we were motoring a mile off-shore looking at the inviting lights of the town of Figueira Da Foz twinkling on the water.

The only movement on the windless ocean was the occasional 'set' of long, silent four foot swells lazily rolling under us from their birth far across the Atlantic. The only other sounds accompanying the low drone of the motor were the periodic faint noises from the distant town.

•

With two years in Ireland behind it, the boat was homeward bound to New England. We were ferrying her from Bayona, Spain, to the Canary Islands. At the islands, laying 100 miles off the coast of Africa, we would rendezvous with my father and Steve Parson for the next leg: the classic transatlantic trade wind sail to the West Indies.

The previous week of combined motoring and sailing had been a mix of pleasure and dirty work. Portugal's old, unpretentious history and welcoming people, plus their terrific bread, delighted and warmed us. But catching up with the multitude of maintenance chores the boat required following two years of use abroad, I could not shake my concern around the problem we were having starting the engine. There was an electrical short-circuit gremlin somewhere. I frequently had to climb down into the engine compartment and manually hot-wire the starter to fire the motor.

Witchery

•

All the sails were furled and the hatches open to the fresh evening air. We were looking for the colored lights that marked the seaward ends of the two long boulder breakwaters that paralleled each other like the paws of a resting dog. Offering good protection for the town's small harbor, these stone sentinels jutted almost a half-mile straight out from shore.

Leaning back against the cushions in the cockpit, Shar sipped from her cup and asked "Isn't it against your rules to enter a strange harbor at night?"

"Ordinarily, yes," I replied, "but considering the calm evening I'm sure we can find the entrance between the two moles and safely run into the inner harbor. That would beat anchoring out here and missing an evening on the town. Besides, on a night like this, how bad could it be?"

It could be, we would learn, a terrifying nightmare that nearly cost both of us our lives.

•

Peering intently into the gloom, we finally spotted the dim red light marking the end of the first mole. Soon followed the profiles of the two great protective barriers looming against the clear, starry sky. The huge, piled boulders created jagged spines that reminded me of guarding dragons. Between them lay a direct line to the distant inner harbor.

The fathometer flashed a comfortable forty-feet of water under us. Rounding the end of the nearest mole we started toward the inviting lights of the town.

Suddenly, the depth alarm intruded on our relaxed confidence. Shar leaned over to check the unit, "That's strange, we only have nine feet under us now." I immediately thought of the river that flowed through the town and imagined a sand bar must have formed at the entrance here—similar to the situation we had chosen to pass up that afternoon. I goosed the throttle and spun the wheel to regain deeper water—something was not right!

Before I could complete the turn, above the laboring engine we heard the frightening sound that every mariner dreads: the nearby deep-throated, roaring rumble of a large breaking wave. Out of the darkness came the source: a six-foot high frothing wave. It hit us just as our turn was almost complete, spraying over the deck and smacking us broadside to what I supposed was the channel.

Shar scrambled below to secure the hatches as I worked to regain control of the boat. My mind mirrored the turmoil around us while I tried to figure out what was happening. Of course! The harmless energy of the benign swells in deep water was being redirected up into these steep waves, tripping and breaking as they contacted the shallow bottom. This must be the beginning of one of the staggered 'sets' we had experienced outside.

The next wave came quickly behind the first. This swell had metamorphosed into a twelve-foot wall of water curling over us. "Hold on tight!" I yelled to Shar bracing myself against the helm. The wave picked the boat up and drove us sideways before exploding over the top, broaching *Witchery* hard on her beam and slapping the masts flat in the water. On impact the main boom launched from its cradle, sheered over and whacked me on the back of the head. For an instant I felt myself somersaulting through the air, perfectly mimicking a crash-test dummy—and then darkness.

•

Below in the cabin, Shar was thrown against the hull as water cascaded over her. She was aghast to find herself sprawled in cold seawater on the galley cabinets. The cabin lights illuminated the chaos of food, books and equipment floating all around her. In a few moments she felt the boat start to rise back onto her keel.

Similarly struggling up, Shar waded through the flotsam securing the last portholes. She then grabbed the radio microphone to send out an emergency call. Looking out of the companionway hatch she went numb. The cockpit where I had been a moment ago was empty! Dropping the mike she clambered towards the upper deck.

•

Only semi-conscious, I noticed blurry colored lights just above me. I needed air badly. Instinctively, I kicked for the lights, surfacing in the frothing whitewater next to the top of the mast. In a dark, surrealistic dream I saw *Witchery* fighting to right herself. Responding to her efforts, the masthead navigation lights beside me started to rise out of the water. My head slowly clearing, I felt the wave driving us towards one of the menacing breakwaters and sensed our margin of space from the rocks quickly disappearing.

I first *heard* the din of another wave charging toward us out of the night, and then *saw* its white crest looming through the darkness, finally taking full menacing shape as it bore down on the boat. It was clear I would be swept away if I didn't reach Shar before it broke. I saw her crawl out of the cabin frantically looking around for me. I was moved by her concern and courage, afraid for us both, but acutely disappointed with myself for breaking the trust my father had placed in me for his boat.

I swam furiously toward her, racing the wave, and grabbed the toe rail just as it overwhelmed the boat and punched the sailboat down flat once again. There was no choice but to grip the rail and roll under with the boat on top of me. My oxygen supply was gone when *Witchery* finally staggered up. Breaking the surface, my face was inches from Shar's on the opposite side of the lifelines. In the first instant she looked surprised, then relief filled her eyes, replaced immediately with determination. She grabbed my collar and shouted "WHERE HAVE YOU BEEN? GET BACK ON THIS BOAT, I NEED YOU!" Exhibiting strength I never imagined from her, she dragged my two hundred drenched pounds into the cockpit. With so much water everywhere, it was hard to tell where the boat ended and the ocean began.

•

At some point in the maelstrom the engine had died. Without it we had little chance of avoiding a quick, violent end— shredded on the rocks like cheese on a grater. Shar jumped back down below, snatched a bucket and started to bail madly. I reached for the key but had faint faith the engine would start.

I was astonished when it caught and fired to life! Engaging the gear, I rammed the throttle full ahead and started to turn into the next breaking sea. My brief instant of hope was shattered when I looked forward and saw that the bow anchor had broken its lashings and was gone! Worse, the anchor chain lay over the bow roller and disappeared into the water. Anchored here we were doomed. I spun around and saw the jagged, wet rocks only yards away, imagining them a monster's spit-glistened teeth eager to have a taste of us.

The valiant boat continued to turn and took the next crashing wave straight on. Another shout to Shar to hang on tight! *Witchery* reared up like a stallion before vanishing under broiling whitewater to her mast winches. She shuddered to a stop, but then surged forward in defiance. I expected to be jerked up short at any moment by the anchor catching below us but, gaining speed, we cleared the moles' maw into deeper water.

As abruptly as they had begun, the waves disappeared. In a moment we were back in deep water and calm ocean. The transition was so dramatic, if not for the water Shar still bailed from the cabin, and my throbbing head, I could have been convinced it had all been a horrible nightmare.

Shar continued to sort out the mess and assess the damage while I ran forward to see about the anchor. In the dim flashlight beam I struggled to believe what I was seeing: The metal thimble joining the chain and anchor-line had jammed sideways in the deck hawse pipe—a slim chance under any circumstances—and the anchor had been denied enough scope to effectively stop us. I knew in my heart what the outcome of the nightmare should have been. The foredeck scene before me blurred as tears filled my eyes. I bowed my head to my knee and marveled at the chances we had been granted and the phenomenal sequence of events leading to our escape.

•

In the days that followed we dried out the boat and found helping hands in a small Portuguese fishing town where we made the repairs necessary to return *Witchery* to seaworthy condition.

Wind, Waves, and a Suicidal Boat

While we worked, both of us continued to wonder at the sense of powerful, unseen helping hands being present that frightening night. Like storms of all kinds, the nightmare, in a paradoxical way, left us with an acute sense of gratitude and wonder. It was a gift that acted to broaden the dimensions of our hearts, and our sense of what is possible.

●●●●●●●●●●

There were other parts to the story I could not escape. I was plagued by a sense of failed responsibility and questioned my self-worth in the aftermath of the decisions that led to our near miss that night. Over the phone my father was gracious and concerned for our health when I related the story to him— but I was less forgiving. As fate, and irony, would have it, I was able to be of use mechanically during the Atlantic crossing— plus, in a wonderful father/son breakthrough for us, we navigated with our sextants across the ocean, shoulder to shoulder, finally coming to a place of mutual respect on the far shore.

EPILOGUE

Much has changed in Bristol Bay since the days when wooden boats sailed the turbulent waters. During most of the 80's and 90's we experienced strong and steady salmon runs, and reasonable prices. Boats got bigger, permits more costly, and debts got higher. The result was a casting aside of the prevailing gentlemen fishery, replaced with a more desperate dog-eat-dog mentality. The focus turned on making payments more than working towards cooperation. But nothing stays the same, and in the late 90's we all experienced a slow- motion slam to the deck of reality: prices dropped, boat and permit values plummeted, and we suddenly became a heavily over-capitalized fishery.

Today, in 2001, we are taking the steps necessary to produce the highest quality product possible. Still, the Alaskan salmon industry faces dark times. Biologically, Alaska has taken great care and expense to ensure that all five species of Pacific salmon return in healthy numbers for future generations. But there are other forces at work. Scientists say we are on the down-slope of what is called the 'decadal oscillation', a natural condition of changing temperatures in the ocean that adversely affects the food chain, and thus the usual abundance of salmon living there. Closer to home, we still have a few international pirates on the high seas intent on harvesting our returning salmon. Russia pushes hard against their furthest 200-mile boundaries to intercept unknown (and perhaps substantial) numbers of Alaskan fish on their homeward journey.

Of major concern is subsidized farmed salmon flooding the world market. While these fish are available year round and have an excellent appearance, they are infused with large quantities of various drugs and growth hormones to keep them disease free; the bland meat is almost always dyed to match the red of the 'wild' fish. That is a subjective consideration for each person to make for themselves.

Of real concern for <u>all</u> of us is the pollution these large fish farms add to pristine waters. The protected bays are often unable to flush clean, killing living things above and below the surface resulting in devastation of the ecosystems where they

93

are grown. Also frightening is the too frequent failure of their containment systems that have freed over a million farmed fish into the ocean. The escapees compete for the food that the wild fish need to survive at critical times. They could easily infect the wild stocks with disease, or worse, interbreed and start an irreversible dilution, perhaps mutation, of the wild salmon gene pool. There is no recovering the purity of the species from a terrible occurrence such as that. We must hold the farmed fish industry accountable for the safety of our precious wild stocks.

•

Alaska strictly regulates the harvest of its bountiful sea life. The intent is for fishermen to harvest only what is sustainable for the future well being of the individual stocks.

Packed with beneficial omega-3, Alaskan wild salmon carries the coveted Marine Stewardship Council's eco-label and, with halibut, are featured prominently as recommended organic fish-of-choice by environmental and health organizations.

•Please enjoy•

THE AUTHOR

Chris White was raised near the sea in New England—one of four children in a boat-loving, seafaring family. Early canoe and skiing expeditions into the Arctic further instilled his love for wild places. After graduating from the University of Colorado, he worked for three years as an instructor at the Minnesota Outward Bound School. He met and married Shar while there. They set off for Alaska early in 1976 in their International Scout and were shoveling herring from the holds of tenders in April; they both had commercial fishing jobs by late spring. After investing in a Bristol Bay limited entry salmon permit in 1977, they started their own commercial fishing business that continues to this day.

Chris has alternately been a lowliner and a highliner in his twenty-five year fishing career. Today he is a respected captain and commercially fishes herring and salmon in Bristol Bay and halibut in the Bering Sea.

Shar still setnets. They both share the joy of their two children, Taran and Tyga, who also fish. Though there is tremendous respect and friendship between them, they are no longer married.

During the winter Chris splits his energy between work and play in the mountains of the northwest, and helping to keep his industry viable and healthy for his children's children.

He can be reached at cwhite@coldreams.com

Order Form

Additional copies of <u>Wind, Waves, and a Suicidal Boat</u> are available from:

<u>The author at:</u>

√**Credit card or check**: cwhite@coldreams.com
                               6015 Baldy Mtn. Rd.
                               Sandpoint, Id. 83864

—or—

√**Phone:** 888-280-7725 / www.1stbooks.com

For Mail Orders

Name:_____

Address:_____

City:_____State:_____Zip:_____

E-mail address:_____

Cost:

<u>**Wind, Waves and a Suicidal Boat**</u> **$11.95** ...._____

Shipping and Handling [first class]
$2.50, [$1.00 each additional copy]   ……………….._____

*Idaho residents add 5% sales tax…………………………*_____

Total…………………………………………………$_____

• [check or money order / 20% discount on 3 or more]

Order Form

Additional copies of <u>Wind, Waves, and a Suicidal Boat</u> are available from:

<u>The author at:</u>

√**Credit card or check**: <u>cwhite@coldreams.com</u>
6015 Baldy Mtn. Rd.
Sandpoint, Id. 83864

—or—

√**Phone:** 888-280-7725 / <u>www.1stbooks.com</u>

<u>For Mail Orders</u>

Name:_____

Address:_____

City:_____State:_____Zip:_____

E-mail address:_____

<u>Cost:</u>

<u>**Wind, Waves and a Suicidal Boat**</u> **$11.95** ………_____

Shipping and Handling [first class]
$2.50, [$1.00 each additional copy] ……………….._____

Idaho residents add 5% sales tax………………………_____

Total……………………………………………….$_____

• [check or money order / 20% discount on 3 or more]

Order Form

Additional copies of <u>Wind, Waves, and a Suicidal Boat</u> are available from:

The author at:

√**Credit card or check**: cwhite@coldreams.com
6015 Baldy Mtn. Rd.
Sandpoint, Id. 83864

—or—

√**Phone:** 888-280-7725 / www.1stbooks.com

For Mail Orders

Name:_____

Address:_____

City:_____State:_____Zip:_____

E-mail address:_____

Cost:

<u>Wind, Waves and a Suicidal Boat</u> **$11.95** ………_____

Shipping and Handling [first class]
$2.50, [$1.00 each additional copy] ……………….._____

*Idaho residents add 5% sales tax…………………………*_____

Total……………………………………………………$_____

• [check or money order / 20% discount on 3 or more]